The Play's the Thing

The Play's the Thing

Promoting Intellectual and Emotional Development in the Early Childhood Years

Selma Wassermann

ROWMAN & LITTLEFIELD
Lanham • Boulder • New York • London

Published by Rowman & Littlefield
An imprint of The Rowman & Littlefield Publishing Group, Inc.
4501 Forbes Boulevard, Suite 200, Lanham, Maryland 20706
www.rowman.com
86-90 Paul Street, London EC2A 4NE, United Kingdom

Copyright © 2023 by Selma Wassermann

All rights reserved. No part of this book may be reproduced in any form or by any electronic or mechanical means, including information storage and retrieval systems, without written permission from the publisher, except by a reviewer who may quote passages in a review.

British Library Cataloguing in Publication Information Available

Library of Congress Cataloging-in-Publication Data

Names: Wassermann, Selma, author.
Title: The play's the thing: promoting intellectual and emotional development in the early childhood years / Selma Wassermann.
Description: Lanham: Rowman & Littlefield, [2023] | Includes bibliographical references. | Summary: "This is a book for teachers and parents as well who seek to develop such self-directed, 'can-do' children"—Provided by publisher.
Identifiers: LCCN 2022057031 (print) | LCCN 2022057032 (ebook) | ISBN 9781475869965 (cloth) | ISBN 9781475869972 (paperback) | ISBN 9781475869989 (epub)
Subjects: LCSH: Moral education (Early childhood) | Play. | Early childhood education—Activity programs.
Classification: LCC LB1139.35.M67 W368 2023 (print) | LCC LB1139.35.M67 (ebook) | DDC 372.21—dc23/eng/20230125
LC record available at https://lccn.loc.gov/2022057031
LC ebook record available at https://lccn.loc.gov/2022057032

For Ruben
the quintessential can-do boy

Contents

Preface	xi
Introduction	xv

SECTION I: BUILDING BLOCKS OF THE "CAN-DO" CHILD ... 1

Chapter 1: Developing Personal Power ... 3

Chapter 2: Building Blocks of Empowerment: Respect for Children and Their Choices ... 7

Chapter 3: Building Blocks of Empowerment: Active Learning Experiences That Genuinely Challenge Children's Thinking ... 13

Chapter 4: Building Blocks of Empowerment: Ensuring Opportunities for Creative, Unsupervised Play ... 17

SECTION II: CLASSROOM APPLICATIONS ... 25

Chapter 5: Introduction to the Activities ... 27

Chapter 6: Debriefing: Using Interactions That Promote Reflection ... 41

Chapter 7: Serious Players: The Arts ... 53

Chapter 8: Serious Players: Language Arts ... 61

Chapter 9: Serious Players: Social Studies ... 79

Chapter 10: Serious Players: Science ... 93

Chapter 11: Serious Players: Math ... 113

Chapter 12: Serious Players: Moral and Ethical Dilemmas ... 131

SECTION III: EPILOGUE — 141

Chapter 13: What's Important? — 143

References — 147

About the Author — 149

If I don't play with it, how can I understand it?

Richard Feynman
Nobel Laureate in Physics

Preface

In the years that we lived dangerously, when a determined and lethal virus wreaked havoc with our lives, we learned many lessons from those terrifying times. We learned how vulnerable we are to infection, despite our twenty-first-century knowledge of science and how to best prevent the spread of germs. We learned that our doctors and nurses, worn to the bone from overwork, went beyond the pale in treating those who fell in such large numbers. We learned to work from home, to use FaceTime and Zoom to connect with family and friends in place of going to the office and visiting others in their homes.

We learned that teaching and learning from home, especially for younger children, was a poor substitute for being in the classroom.

The impact of those years of self-quarantine taught us that we needed to depend on our own inner resources to keep us not only safe but emotionally healthy. We were not able to enjoy the recreational activities that we regularly used to give us pleasure. Movies, playgrounds, gyms, restaurants, schools were not safe nor available. We had to rely on not only what we could find between the walls of our own homes and perhaps gardens, but also to seek, within ourselves, the means and the resources to enlighten, amuse, educate, and give us some feeling of stability.

Adults who were not accustomed to finding such inner resources were hard put to find their comfort zones. Many succumbed to depression. Hardest hit were the children, who, without the systematic daily schedules that schools offered, sought time-occupying activities in tablets, TVs, and computer games. These were hardly enough to keep them happy. Parents, who were already stressed by the conditions of quarantine, had to assume the full-time job of looking after the children and seeing to their emotional and academic needs.

The sad results were seen in the ways too many children were responding: depression, high anxiety, acting out, and desperate loneliness. Many feared that children would not quickly recover from such long-term deprivations.

Yet there were some children who did not suffer in the same ways. There were parents who found ways, despite the various limitations that the quarantine imposed, to engage them, to ensure they were purposefully occupied, to supply the conditions that, despite being homebound, gave each day a fresh and sparkling sheen. These children came away from their two-year quarantine minus the scars and the trauma that many other children suffered, happily ready to return to school without learning loss.

What was the difference? What accounted for the different outcomes in these two disparate groups?

The early childhood years are of the greatest importance in shaping the characters of children. How parents and teachers build character, how they contribute to "can-do" or "can't-do" children, is at the heart of this book. These "building blocks" consist, fundamentally, in the ways parents and teachers talk to children and in the ways they supply the conditions that lead to the development of greater personal autonomy. In other words, the difference between "can-do" and "can't-do" kids.

In another century, children were more or less left to their own devices. They had more unsupervised time to play, to engage with their peer groups out of doors, whether they lived in cities or in the suburbs or on farms. The IT world was the stuff of science fiction; TV programs that were child-oriented were carefully parceled out by parents who understood the draw of such commercial seductions. Parents were less fearful that children going outside to play with friends put them in danger.

What such unsupervised play taught children was to make up their own rules and to enforce them. It taught them the skills necessary to engage in social cooperation in all kinds of social spaces. It taught them the skills of problem solving and cooperation. It taught them that they had to rely on their own resources and to create their own conditions for engagement with their peers (Horwitz 2015). Unsupervised play gave children almost unlimited opportunity to exercise choice and to deal with the consequences of those choices. Such opportunities to choose empowered them as autonomous individuals. Unstructured free play was an important developmental key to their becoming self-directed, "can-do" kids.

In recent generations, childhood has become more tightly circumscribed with less opportunity for unsupervised free time. Children's activities are more rigorously programmed, with more at-home time spent online and with other IT "toys." There is hardly any time for free, unstructured play, for unsupervised time inside or outside of the home.

Schools, as well, have been major contributors in creating more outer-directed children since most, if not all, school activities are strictly scheduled and operate on a defined time line. In some primary school programs, even young children spend time on workbook exercises, sitting at their desks, and waiting for teachers to tell them what to do, how to do it, and how much time they have to finish the job.

Such a shift in the ethos of child-rearing has contributed, to a large extent, to impeding the development of children's effective self-governance. Instead of growing to become more self-directed, where they are freer to make their own choices of what to do and how, children's time is now rigorously programmed. Even their play with other children has been scheduled as "play dates."

Because unsupervised free play is nature's way of teaching us the skills we need as adults—the skills of cooperation, making and enforcing rules, compromise, negotiating conflicts, accepting defeat—children have become dependent on others to regulate them. More and more they have become "other directed." It is no surprise then that during the days of self-quarantine, when schools, playgrounds, and other recreational activities were shut down, children were subject to the emotional stresses of having to find their own way. Their self-direction, having had little chance of development, failed them when they needed it most.

When teachers and parents legislate and structure children's lives in ways that make it harder for children to develop a sense of self-direction, we take away from them a key "building block" of what makes it possible for them to grow into self-directed adults. Such children will always be dependent on others to tell them what to do, what to think, how to behave. They will look to others for directing their actions instead of looking within themselves.

There is great danger in such skewed development, not only for a peaceful and productive social order but also for one's own emotional well-being.

And that, alas, is more than likely to account for the differences in these groups of children. Those who have a strong sense of self-direction, of personal autonomy, used their time to invent, create, read, and play, enjoying those degrees of freedom to make their own choices.

This is a book for teachers and parents who seek to develop such self-directed, "can-do" children.

Introduction

The experiences adults provide for children in their early childhood years are of singular importance in shaping the people they later become. The experiences that contribute to children's intellectual and emotional development are found, to a large extent, in the ways children are treated—by their parents, their peers, their schools, and their culture. In short, by all the experiences children have and the ways each contributes to the shaping of their individual selves.

In providing these early childhood experiences, it would be fair to say that no parent or teacher desires that children become "can't-do" kids, dependent on outside sources to guide them, to tell them what to do and how, to do their thinking for them. The evidence suggests, however, that there is a huge gap between parents' and teachers' hopes and aspirations and children's lived experiences at home and in school. How this gap occurs is one of the important issues addressed in this book.

In the first section of the book, the theoretical foundations for the development of "can-do" kids are identified. These include the importance of unstructured, unsupervised free play for their social, psychological, and intellectual development; the emotional need for personal power; the gratification that active learning experiences bring to children's feelings of self-worth; and finally, the imperative of respect for children and for their choices.

The position taken in these beginning chapters is that, when certain conditions exist in homes and in schools, children are empowered. They grow in their feelings of self-respect, self-worth, and intellectual competence. Therein lie the essentials of their "can-do" spirit. No one who is deeply concerned with the healthful development of children will reject these ideas.

Who, after all, will be the first to say that children's play is bad? Or that children should not be intellectually challenged? Or that they should not be treated respectfully? That is what parents and teachers want for children. And we want this in our homes and in our school programs.

Woven together, these developmental theories provide the foundation for the building of those self-directed characteristics that are so essential to autonomous, thoughtful, can-do adults. This is opposite to the "learned helplessness" that was seen in so many children during their time away from schools. An examination of the research about learned helplessness reveals a startling relationship between such feelings and susceptibility to illness and disease (Seligman 1991).

How teachers and parents may provide the conditions to enable empowerment is at the heart of this book. Six chapters include dozens of activities that show how play becomes the basis for intellectual development in the curriculum areas of social studies, math, language arts, art and music, and science. Chapter 6 describes how parent-child and teacher-child conversations contribute to empowerment and how other kinds of conversations diminish children's sense of autonomy.

These first two sections provide not only a theoretical basis for the development of "can-do" kids but also include practical help to teachers and parents in bringing about these important goals of child growth and development.

In the last section, issues related to the dilemmas of choosing and the importance of play for adults are discussed, winding up with the question that teachers and parents need to ask themselves in providing the growing conditions that enable children: what's important? Only when adults know this for themselves can they chart the courses that will align their actions with their goals.

A book is never the work of a single author, and in this text, acknowledgment is gratefully made to the several people whose work contributed to the author's thinking and to the creation of the materials within. First and foremost, to the estimable Richard Feynman, a most serious player, who claimed that his work with tossing dinner plates up in the air to observe their spin led him to receive the Nobel Prize in Physics. He never underestimated the power of play to enrich personal understanding of complicated concepts, shifting our notion of play from the frivolous to the essential in learning, not only for children but for adults as well.

The work of Sylvia Ashton-Warner must also be included for giving life to the notion of the importance of creative play in the primary grades. Ashton-Warner was among the few who described how play not only broadened children's creative capabilities but also served to promote cooperation, problem solving, and critical thinking skills.

My appreciation, too, to Kai and Maya Snow and their mom, Lin Snow, for their permission to include photos of them at play, and to Lin Snow for her permission to use the spice activity and the Cookie Stand.

Many thanks, as well, to Rich Mooney for the photo on the cover of the book, and to Ruben for giving his permission to use the photo.

To Christiana Brianik, at Teachers College Press, I owe a debt of gratitude for her help in securing permissions to re-create for this book material from the previously published *Serious Players in the Primary Classroom*.

To my main man, the wizard of Parksville, Simon Snow, for his expert IT help, without which I'd still be writing with a pencil on a yellow pad.

To those first "serious players" Simon and Arlo, from whom I learned about unsupervised, unstructured play in situ, who have retained their sense of play as dads with their own children.

And not least to my publisher, Tom Koerner, and the editorial staff at Rowman & Littlefield, my warmest thanks and gratitude for your support of my work.

SECTION I

Building Blocks of the "Can-Do" Child

Chapter 1

Developing Personal Power

The word *power* has a bad reputation. When we think of power, we generally think of it in its negative sense. We associate it with unpleasant feelings and actions, with needs to dominate, control, and exert influence over others. Power has decidedly good sides, however. For example, the power of a play to move an audience to tears; the power of an orator to stir; the power of an idea to inspire action. The sense of satisfaction one experiences from an extraordinary accomplishment—reaching the mountaintop after a long and arduous climb—is also related positively to power.

This sense of *power-to*—what we feel as a result of something accomplished for our own satisfaction—feeds the ego. The message given to the self is, "I can do this! There is something special about me!"

It is true that a person who sits in a seat of power and exerts power over others is much to be feared and despised. We have seen numerous examples of the use of violence and cruelty in the exercise of power over others. The current example of Russia's brutal invasion of Ukraine is one more instance of an authoritarian regime exercising power over a smaller nation in order to bend that country to its knees. In almost every circumstance the exercise of power over others means the use of resources to control the freedoms of others for personal satisfaction or gain (French 1985).

Power-to, on the other hand, increases personal satisfaction. It is related to ego strength, self-confidence, and heightened personal autonomy. People with a well-developed sense of power-to are able to "be in charge of their lives." Carl Rogers (1961) has called these adults "fully functioning." We have seen how they operate in our professional circles, among our friends, and in the marketplace of life, and we admire them. There is a positive spirit about them, a sense of "can-do."

In tough situations, they are able to take charge, and their actions reveal thoughtful and intelligent procedures. When faced with a problem requiring some innovative action, they do not shirk but rather embrace the problem with positive energy. We trust them to find solutions. Their confidence in themselves fills us with confidence in them.

A very good example of such a person is Richard Feynman. That he won the Nobel Prize in Physics is only one indication of his extraordinary can-do spirit. What is even more extraordinary is that he lived with an unshakable belief in his own capability to do, which allowed him to take on tasks far outside his own area of expertise. Music (drumming) and painting were just two of his other skills, requiring quite diverse talents, and he succeeded in doing them with remarkable ease.

When Feynman was faced with a problem that required an immediate solution and for which he had no previously developed skill, he invariably began with a positive attitude about his potential for finding a solution. Inevitably he found one (Feynman 1985).

What kinds of growth conditions contribute to the development of power-to? How can children grow to believe in themselves with such confidence? How is such positive growth turned inside out, resulting instead in an insatiable need for power over others? What's the relationship between power-over and power-to?

THE ROOTS OF POWER-CONTROL THEORY

There is some reason to believe that the development of a sense of personal power is an emotional needs derivative. Like our basic human needs for love, belonging, and economic security, we may also have the need for power-to inherent in our human makeup. Glasser, in his book *Control Theory in the Classroom* (1985), tells us that "all of our behavior is always our best attempt to satisfy at least five powerful forces which, because they are built into our genetic structure, are best called basic needs." One is the need to stay alive and reproduce; the other four, all psychological needs, are "belonging (which includes love), power, freedom and fun." Everything we do may thus be seen as aimed at satisfying one or more of these needs.

Children who grow up in environments in which they are loved, where they feel they belong, and where they feel safe and emotionally secure become emotionally healthy adults. Children who grow up in environments in which there is little or no emotional nurturance grow up "haywire," with very little chance of their becoming emotionally whole adults. In very extreme cases, loss of such nurturing has even resulted in the tragic deaths of otherwise healthy babies (Spitz 1949).

Serious neglect of a child's emotional needs may result in maladaptive behaviors that present grave problems for the child, the family and the community at large. The data suggest that the potential and likely results of emotional needs deprivation include extreme forms of aggression, obedient submissiveness, withdrawal, acute psychosomatic symptoms of illness, and regression to more primitive forms of behavior (Raths 1969, 1998; Wassermann 1991).

If the development of a sense of personal power or power-to is seen as one more important emotional need, it also follows that it must be adequately satisfied in the early years of childhood if children are to grow into adults who believe in their own capabilities: can-do adults. Power-to needs are fed when adults allow children choices, when even very young children exercise their own options in situations that genuinely matter to them. Allowing children choices implicitly communicates that we believe in them and in their ability to make those decisions. When they are given options, when they are allowed to choose, when their choices are respected, they grow to believe in themselves. They learn that they can do.

A sense of can-do and feelings of personal power are thus intimately connected. Children learn to believe that they have power to make a change, that they have control over their environment. It is not certain why, but it is clear that exercising one's power-to is enormously satisfying. This is seen with even the youngest children, who wish to make their owns choices and who, when choice is given, are satisfied, even elated. Underlying all of this is of course the respect that is part and parcel of allowing children choices. This is such a fundamental condition that it hardly needs mentioning. But it is, alas, too often absent from observable adult-child behaviors.

When the power to choose is taken away by others who exercise control, children become frustrated, even enraged. Kohn (1998) cites apathy and disengagement as well as thoughtlessness and aggression as behavioral symptoms of powerlessness, which results when adults exercise control over most of children's actions. By virtue of such adult behavior, children learn that they are not to be trusted. They learn not that they can do but that they can't do. The absence of respect for them and for their choices leaves them with feelings of doubt, uncertainty, and lack of self-worth.

When children's drives for power-to continue to be thwarted, they are likely to show increased frustration and anger that is manifest in acts of extreme aggression. It is no wonder that adults with frustrated power-to needs desire power-over.

Power-over needs are compensatory in that they seek to make up for personal power deficits. They are also ways of acting out feelings of aggression. Maladaptive behaviors resulting from power-to needs deficits may take a variety of forms. The most extreme include those bizarre acts of aggression and terrorism we read about in newspapers and in history books, such as those committed by torturers, secret police forces, the Ku Klux Klan, terrorist groups, dictators, and, lamentably, children with guns. In all these cases, bodily harm, violence, and destruction become the route to power-over needs satisfaction. The more moderately aggressive forms of maladaptive behavior include that of "highly controlling" adults in positions of power who maintain control over the options of others.

There are also the mildly aggressive forms, expressed in the need for heavy-duty motorcycles or noisy, intrusive radios, where the user can unleash a surge of power on the environment and its inhabitants. Whether mild or extreme, the message is the same: "Look at me! I have power!" What that indicates is a desperate need to demonstrate power through external force and an acute lack of confidence that true power resides within.

Other subtle forms of behavior suggesting personal power deficits are found in the relentless acquisition of "power toys"—the key to the executive washroom, higher positions in power hierarchies, expensive cars, homes in fashionable or exclusive areas, designer clothes. These more subtle power trappings supposedly make a person feel more powerful, yet such extreme needs to demonstrate power signal inner deficits.

Unsatisfied needs for power-to can never be adequately met through power-over actions. A person caught up in a power-over drive may seek to increase a power-over base but will never be adequately satisfied. The more one has, the more one wants, in a never-ending quest to satisfy an unquenchable thirst.

While aggressive behaviors are one manifestation of inadequately satisfied power-to drives, at the other end of the behavior spectrum are those teens and adults who have given up. For whatever reasons, aggression has given way to obedient submission. As children, many of these teens and adults learned habits of obedience, bowing to others' commands and turning to them to be "in charge" of them. Their courage to try, to take risks, and to decide for themselves has been diminished. Fear of doing has become part of their essence.

Instead of an inner core of "can-do," of personal power, they are burdened with an overwhelming sense of personal defeat. Their handicaps make them vulnerable to the power-over ploys of others. In any circumstance where you see obedient submission to a dominant, controlling authority, you see examples of grown-ups who have been disempowered.

The gamut of these submissive behaviors extends from the obedient and docile wife who must ask permission from her husband for any decision of consequence to the incomprehensible suicides of the scores of adults and children who were ordered to take their lives by the "Reverend" Jim Jones. Seligman (1991) refers to this behavior as learned helplessness.

People who have developed a sense of personal power, whose feelings of can-do are strong and highly developed, have little need to acquire power trappings for reassurance. Individuals who feel empowered do not need to exercise power over others nor allow others to control their lives.

Chapter 2

Building Blocks of Empowerment
Respect for Children and Their Choices

I'm not little. I'm four.

Adults—parents, teachers and significant others, are the people who are largely responsible for the healthful development of young children. Like growing flowers, where certain conditions are essential to produce beautiful blossoms (e.g., good quality soil, sunlight, water, fertilizer, proper temperature), adults provide the conditions that are the growing grounds for empowered children. These conditions include, at the very first, provision for children's physical safety and well-being, as well as emotional nurturance, respect for children as persons and for their right to exercise their own choices, opportunities for active engagement in tasks that challenge their thinking, and opportunities for creative, unstructured play.

It is with these last three conditions—building blocks of personal power—that this and the following two chapters are concerned.

RESPECTING CHILDREN AS PERSONS AND RESPECTING THEIR CHOICES

"Even infants and toddlers are people worthy of respect." (Lansbury 2022)

While physical safety and emotional nurturance stand at the head of any list of essential growth conditions for children, treating them with respect takes its place the very top as well. It is when children feel respected that they strengthen that aspect of personhood upon which all healthful psychological growth rests: self-respect. Empowerment derives from self-respect; the absence of self-respect diminishes us.

Respect is shown when children receive recognition for who they are and what they do. Respect is also shown when children are allowed to choose for themselves, that is, when they are allowed to make decisions affecting their lives and when their decisions are acknowledged and valued. In this way we show respect for their right to function on their own, apart from us, as separate, able persons. Children who are allowed to make their own choices grow to see themselves as capable persons who can positively influence the environment in which they live.

They learn to see themselves as persons of worth.

This is not to suggest, of course, that children should have unlimited choices about everything they do; that would be absurd. We should not allow choices in life-threatening situations, nor should we allow choice where certain options are unwise or unwarranted or simply inappropriate. Children may still have control over their choices when they are choosing from among appropriate options.

Respect for children is not shown by deferential treatment, by fawning, by patronizing them, by telling them that what they know to be true is false. Respect is not shown through excessive praise for everything a child does. On the contrary, excessive praise is likely to be as harmful as overt neglect, for it is phony.

Respect is shown through interactions that attend thoughtfully to what children have to say, through our attempts to understand what they are telling us and how they feel, and through our nonjudgmental acceptance of those feelings and thoughts. Respect is shown through interactions that are genuine. The communication of respect for children is not different from how adults communicate respect for each other.

Primary classrooms and homes that routinely provide many opportunities for children to choose, to decide on matters of substance, are places where they have greater opportunities to increase their sense of personal power. Here's how respect for children in a grade one class might appear:

The class is choosing activities for the morning's free play time. One by one the children make a choice from the following activity centers: puzzles, reading, drawing, blocks, mosaics, Lego, painting. When a choice has been made, each child then moves to that activity center. It's Ruben's turn to choose, and he picks Lego. It is the fifth time in a row that he has chosen Lego, and the teacher has a moment of concern that he may be limiting his play experiences to a single activity. How does his teacher communicate these concerns yet show respect for Ruben's choice?

"You must really love Lego, Ruben. You keep choosing it again and again."

Or, "Lego is always your first choice, Ruben. You don't seem to want to choose anything else."

In either response, Ruben's choice is respected and treated courteously. Both responses implicitly ask Ruben to think about that choice in relation to other options. Both allow Ruben to have the final say about his choice.

Disrespect for Ruben's choice is shown by rejecting it, by manipulating him, by taking away his option to choose:

"Ruben, you have had five turns at Lego this week. It's time for you to choose another activity."

Or, "Now, Ruben, don't you think you've had enough Lego for this week? Don't you think you should try something else?"

Or, "You haven't been to puzzles yet, Ruben, so you'd better go there today. You can't do Lego all the time."

Communicating and showing respect for children occurs when adults can let go of their need to persuade children that they must always be obedient to our directives, that we know better than they what they need, what is good for them, what activities are more suitable for their play, how much time they need to complete a task. When Claudia says, "I'm tired now. I don't want to do this work anymore," and her teacher urges, "You must finish it," or her parent presses, "Just do a little more," or, "You can't go out to play unless you finish," they are communicating neither respect for the child's feelings nor acceptance of what she has said as having validity.

Such manipulation of children disempowers them.

It is easy to be disrespectful of young children. They are physically smaller than we are, and if push comes to shove, we have the upper hand. They have less ability to control their needs, and their needs, wants, and drives can be exceedingly tiresome. Because they have less experience, they need lengthier and more in-depth explanations, and this is especially annoying when adults are in a hurry (which we are a lot of the time). We attribute to children the need to be told, to be shown, to be directed, and to have their lives happily organized by us. And we believe that we have the right to do these things because we are smarter, know more, and know better what is best for them.

It is easy for us to manipulate children, to get them to do what we want them to do or think they *should* do. And lots of adults exercise such power over children a lot of the time. But the rewards we reap from such behavior, from such disempowerment, are grim. What's more, through such actions, we have given children powerful role models of how to behave as adults.

Listening to adults talk to children in different settings reveals how disrespect habitually occurs:

- Alan, age six, shinnies up a supporting pole and begins traversing the horizontal ladder hand over hand, his small body twisting under the physical stress of the activity. He goes to the fourth rung and then drops about six feet to the ground with a gasp. His father, watching, yells for the world to hear: "What's the matter with you, Alan? Your brother can do better than that!"

- Sonia, age five, is sitting with her parents, waiting for the whale show to begin at the aquarium. They have been waiting for more than fifteen minutes, and Sonia is beginning to be restless. She starts to kick her feet out in a rhythmic pattern, expressing some of her frustration. Her mother reproaches, "You can't be taken anywhere! Stop that at once. That's the last time I'm taking you anywhere."
- Brian is reluctant to enter the pool area at the playground. This is his first time here, and he knows none of the other children. His father urges, "Don't be a baby. Get in there. There's nothing to be afraid of."
- Zita requests permission to go to the bathroom, and her teacher admonishes that she should have gone during recess, that she can't just go to the bathroom whenever she wants.
- Malcolm hasn't finished his worksheet in the allotted time, and he is told by his teacher that he has been wasting his time and not trying his best.

It is easy to forget, as these negative judgments slip from our mouths, the power of such statements to undermine and diminish children's self-respect, to make them unsure of themselves, doubtful, undermined. It is easy to forget, in our drive to *teach* children our way, that we may, in fact, be teaching them other lessons—that they are not capable, not worthy of our thoughtful consideration, not entitled to our respect for them and for their immediate needs. We may, in our words and deeds, be chipping away at those building blocks of empowerment.

CONCLUSION

Parents, teachers and other significant adults play pivotal roles in building children's respect for themselves. And for some children, these adults can play *the* pivotal role. For, even as we must not underestimate children, so we may not underestimate the power of a parent, a teacher, a significant adult to breathe new life into children and to empower them for all their lives.

When we think about our own parents, teachers, and significant others, particularly those who have been singular forces that shaped us as adults, we inevitably think of those memorable people who empowered us. If we remember what they did and how they did it, and why we remember them above all others, we will recall that they respected us, that they seemed to understand how we felt, that they recognized and appreciated who we were and what we did, that they asked for our ideas and listened to them with serious consideration. They were always genuine in their behavior to us, never phony.

These adults increased, rather than crushed, our choices. When such respect is shown for children's persons and their choices, self-respect grows. Children who grow up under conditions where they are respected are empowered. They have the internal tools to become can-do kids.

Chapter 3

Building Blocks of Empowerment

Active Learning Experiences That Genuinely Challenge Children's Thinking

Please mom. I want to do my own thinking.

A second condition in the empowerment of young children is providing for their active engagement with tasks that are a genuine challenge to their thinking. Such experiences begin at early stages of life, even in the crib. A mother pulls a rattle out and shakes it, and the baby responds by turning toward and reaching for it. Grabbing the rattle is a challenging task for an infant. She must process some data before she is able to connect hand with rattle. When she has performed this task, the mother makes her acknowledgment and regard explicit.

"What a smart girl you are!" The baby smiles. Though she may not comprehend the language, the tone of voice and the look on the mother's face tell the baby the entire story of delight in the accomplishment.

In toddler years, we give children other active learning tasks that challenge: puzzles to assemble, blocks to build with, balls to throw and catch, beads to string. We also invite them to help with the household chores: putting enough spoons on the table, fetching three potatoes from the bin, finding the matching shoe in the closet, holding the dustpan under the swept-up crumbs. Children seek and need active engagement in age-appropriate activities that challenge them. When we allow for and encourage this, we are building feelings of empowerment, of a can-do spirit, of personal satisfaction in their own achievements.

As children grow, we encourage them with more complex and more sophisticated active learning challenges: punching in the right numbers on a phone, tying shoelaces, finding a can of tomatoes in the pantry, filling the dog's water bowl. We encourage them to engage in problem-solving situations that require concrete and abstract processing, that call for developing new skills, understandings, and meanings. In these challenges to their problem-solving abilities, a critical dimension is that of active, purposeful engagement. In every task, there is a real need for the task to be done, and the child is aware of this.

The challenge must not be contrived if it is to retain its significance as a challenge. It must also be developmentally appropriate, neither too simple nor excessively beyond the child's reach, if it is to be effective in building a sense of personal power. In almost every case, such challenges require children's experiential involvement in the task. It is not enough for them simply to listen to explanations of how it should be done. They must do it themselves. Through repeated, everyday experiences with such tasks, children learn habits of thinking and gain confidence in themselves as thinkers, as problem solvers. Such confidence builds feelings of personal power, of "I can do."

When children come to school, they face other challenges, some of which have very little to do with building feelings of empowerment. They may be challenged to sit for long periods of time, to sit in confined places without a lot of wriggling, to be silent. They may be challenged to follow a school schedule that is not in harmony with their own organic growing needs, to obey and do as they are told, to eat food that they do not like, to perform bodily functions on schedule rather than out of physical need. They may be challenged to complete tasks that have little meaning for them, to say they enjoy activities that bore them, to pretend to be interested in books and stories that are substantially dull.

None of these challenges, unfortunately, contributes to empowerment, nor does any of them provide any real challenge to young children's higher-order thinking skills. In fact, the opposite is true: such tasks train them to be obediently submissive, to do as they are told, to bow to power over them.

Teachers can do a great deal to empower children as they provide them with opportunities to engage in real activities that challenge their thinking. In Heather McAllister's kindergarten classroom, students have been grouped for investigative play with science materials. She has gathered the materials to be used and placed them where children can get to them easily. In one group the children are carrying out investigations with prisms. They are designing increasingly sophisticated inquiries that start with, "I wonder what would happen if . . . ?" In another group they are making observations of three eggs—one that is fresh, one that has been immersed in a vinegar solution for two days, and another that has been immersed in a vinegar solution for two weeks.

The children decide how their investigations are to be conducted, how and when to break the eggs, how to examine them, and what to look for. These investigations are genuine challenges for them. They learn habits of thinking as they figure out ways to test hypotheses and interpret data, while creating new investigations. In each situation, children are actively involved in learning tasks. It is the children who are doing the thinking, rather than sitting and listening to the teacher's thinking.

The teacher is on the periphery of these activities. She has given over control of the learning operations to the children. While she is never far away, psychologically or physically, she does not take direct action in the children's investigations. She is there to answer questions if they arise or to intervene to deal with crises and lend psychological support. Otherwise, she does not direct what the students are learning. In allowing them to create and take on these challenges, Heather provides the conditions in which they grow in personal power. In that way, she is creating the building blocks in their development of personal power.

In Kim Kaslo's grade one class, children are routinely challenged by his whole language program. Their writing and reading skills grow as children exercise choice over what books they read and what stories they write in their journals. They are challenged by working as writers do, in reviewing their stories and in making the corrections they believe necessary. Kim's language arts program is a genuine challenge to children's thinking. As children grow in their capability to take on these challenges, they develop habits of thinking. When thinking skills are strengthened, children are empowered.

Lin Snow, a mom at home, had to take charge when her daughter, age nine, and her son, age six, were homebound during the COVID school closings. She made certain that many manipulative materials were easily available to give both a chance to become actively involved with creative play tasks: blocks, crayons, pastels, lots of paper for drawing, writing and coloring; measuring tools; a bin of old clothes for dress up; rag doll puppets; and lots and lots of books. When the children had reached the end of their tolerance for the materials available, she created an "I'm Bored" jar containing children's ideas on slips of paper for what they could do when they "felt bored."

When Kai had reached the end of his patience for his play with his Keva bricks, he didn't have to announce that he "was bored." He just went to the "I'm Bored" jar, pulled out an idea, thought about it, and then set to work on a new activity.

Even stuck at home and away from school, Lin made sure to provide many opportunities for Maya and Kai to be actively involved in activities that challenged their thinking and increased their sense of "can-do."

Chapter 4

Building Blocks of Empowerment
Ensuring Opportunities for Creative, Unsupervised Play

The pendulum of educational reform swings from left to right and back again with an almost circadian rhythm. When those in power positions over school curricula come from more traditional schools of thought, reforms shift classroom activities and organizations to the far right. If those in leadership positions come from more progressive schools of thought, reforms then shift to the left, to more modern, more innovative practices. These shifts occur with nauseating frequency, with teachers caught up in the latest organizational schemes du jour, no matter their own more intelligent and informed perspectives on what methods, activities, and organizations are best for their own students.

Children's play, once believed to be essential in the healthful growth and development of young children, did not escape these pendulum swings. When more traditional practices reigned, schools saw "innovations" in the form of "teaching to behavioral objectives," the No Child Left Behind Act, the Common Core State Standards, and "time on task"—each with heavy emphasis on standardized testing that used evaluation to measure and rank students, much to the dismay of teachers, parents, and children caught in the never-ending pressure of performing to mandated standards.

Play was anathema, a waste of children's time, as teachers struggled to get them ready for the next set of tests. Those who benefited most from these reforms were the test makers, who reaped the most in financial gains.

More humane and more child-centered organizational schemes came from sources like the British Primary School Program (1971) and led to more open classrooms and more emphasis on students' active engagement in learning activities. Play was featured as an essential component of early childhood education. The British Primary School Program made clear the dynamic interface of children's play and inquiry-type learning, collapsing the traditional view of work and play as separate entities in the cognitive development of children.

In describing his experiences observing the British Primary School Program, Featherstone (1971) explained:

> There are no individual desks and no assigned places. Around the room there are different tables for different activities: art, water and sand play, number work. The number tables have all kinds of number lines . . . strips of paper with numbers marked on them in sequence; on these children learn to count and reason mathematically. There are beads, buttons and odd things to count; weights and balances; dry and liquid measures; and a rich variety of apparatus for learning basic mathematical concepts, some of it home-made, some ready-made.
>
> The best of the commercial materials are familiar; Cuisenaire rods, the Dienes multibase material, Stern rods and attribute or logical blocks. This sort of thing is stressed much more than formal arithmetic. Every room has a Wendy House—a play corner with dolls and furniture for playing house. Often there is a dress up corner too. Some classes have puppet theaters; in the integrated day there is no demarcation of subjects, or between work and play.

IN SUPPORT OF PLAY

Jonathan Haidt (2022), writing in his forceful essay "How Social Media Dissolved the Mortar of Society and Made America Stupid," pointed to the fact that

> childhood today has become more tightly circumscribed, with less opportunity for free, unstructured play; less unsupervised time outside, more time online. Whatever else the effects of these shifts, they have likely impeded the development of abilities needed for effective self-governance for many young adults. Unsupervised free play is nature's way of teaching young mammals the skills they'll need as adults, which for humans include the ability to cooperate, make and enforce rules, compromise, adjudicate conflicts and accept defeat.

The economist Steven Horwitz (2015) argued that free play prepares children for the art of association that Alexis de Tocqueville claimed was the key to the vibrancy of American democracy. He also argued that its loss posed a serious threat to liberal societies. A generation prevented from learning these social skills, Horowitz warned, would habitually appeal to authorities to resolve disputes and would suffer from a coarsening of social interaction that would create a world of more conflict and violence.

Sylvia Ashton-Warner (1963) has written that creativity is on the other side of the human coin from destructivity. She pointed out that in children both creative and destructive impulses are found side by side. One side is enlarged at the expense of constricting the other. In other words, destructive children rarely create. They spend their energies aggressively violating persons and property. Yet this can be turned around, for as we begin to tap that creative side, destructive impulses are diminished.

Children today have far fewer opportunities to engage in active, unsupervised play. In the place of traditional childhood games, in the place of fantasy and make-believe play, today's children have video games, tablets, and the Wide World Web. With such limited opportunity to tap a child's creative imagination and with such counterproductive forces in motion, what kinds of adults are today's children likely to become? And what kind of world are they likely to create?

The data are unequivocally on the side of play. Bettelheim (1987), writing in the *Atlantic*, reminds us that play is a means for children to cope with concerns that are pressing on their minds and hearts, the most useful tool for preparing them for the future, for the tasks that lie ahead of them.

Jerome Bruner (1985), cognitive psychologist and professor emeritus at Harvard University, conducted extensive studies of young children at play. His data should be enough to convince even the most die-hard skeptics that the imperative of children's play has been borne out by empirical investigation:

> There is evidence that by getting children to play with materials that they must later use in problem solving tasks, one gets superior performance from them in comparison with those children who spend time familiarizing themselves with the materials in various other ways. The players generate more hypotheses and they reject wrong ones more quickly. They seem to become frustrated less and fixated less. (Bruner 1985)

THE PLAY'S THE THING

The development and nurturing of the more self-directed child come from their engagement in play—the primary avenue of development that provides them with the greatest opportunities for inner direction. No one has to tell them what to do, how to do it, and how much time they have to do it in. All of these controls are exercised as part of what they do. When opportunities for creative play are substantially reduced, children look to others to exercise the controls for directing their lives.

As children grow in their self-directed behaviors, flexibility, risk-taking capabilities, and tolerance for dissonance and inventiveness, they grow in their belief in themselves, in their belief that they can accomplish whatever they set out to do. As a consequence, they grow in personal power (Isenberg and Quisenberry 1988).

The data in support of play, while sufficiently compelling, still do not cover all the advantages of play. It is, in fact, a many splendored thing. Play is the main source of our creativity. The majestic breakthroughs, the real masterpieces of invention throughout history, have come from the creative thinking of the most fertile, inventive minds, minds that play with ideas as children play with ideas in their experiential play. Such creators behave very much as young children. Driven by endless curiosity and not satisfied to accept conventional wisdom, they are given to testing, experimenting, and exploring.

Every teacher who has watched children play knows, too, that play is a humanizer. As they play, children work through a variety of interpersonal and social problems. "Who will be first? "Why should I give up my turn?" "When will it be my turn?" "I don't want to share!" "Bobby has my truck." "I don't want to play with her." "She's not being nice to me." "She wants my ball."

In play, real emotions are expressed, and through play, we learn to tap those emotions and manage them. In these ways we grow more multidimensional. Play allows us the full gamut of emotions—joy, pleasure, pain, frustration, anger, exhilaration. It may be the only in-school experience in which emotions are naturally expressed. Through play there is genuine, spontaneous laughter. Can we have more laughter in our classrooms without the feeling that we are producing a crop of idlers?

We have all seen adults who have lost their spontaneity and consequently their ability to play. Instead of real play, they engage in directed and controlled play-type activities, such as organized sports and games. But what is emphasized in these activities is not so much pleasure but competition. "Is this a fun game or a winning game?" a four-year-old asks, who easily discerns the difference.

We have also seen adults who try to legislate play at parties or in other group gatherings. Some of them have to consume quantities of alcohol before they can "let go" of their play inhibitions. Often the resulting behavior is more tragic than joyful, to all parties concerned.

Adults who have lost the joy and spontaneity of play have a missing human dimension. They may be smart, successful, competent; they may have a lot of power over and many power toys. But they live out their lives bereft of the single human trait that brings the greatest capacity for pleasure in their lives.

If we have cultivated the art of play early in our lives, we are likely to hold onto our self-initiating behaviors, our capacity for risk taking, our inventiveness as adults. We are less likely to have to spend our considerably increased leisure time watching game shows on TV, playing video games, or spending endless hours with social media because we have not developed our self-directing resources.

Teachers who consistently provide opportunities for free, unsupervised, unstructured play in their early childhood classrooms contribute substantially to the healthful social, cognitive, and psychological empowering of more self-directed children.

WHAT CAN PARENTS DO?

During the very stressful months of self-quarantine, when children were kept out of school and parents bore the full brunt of looking after their health and welfare 24/7, the effects of such isolation were seen in reports of children becoming ill with various symptoms of anxiety and depression. Children, who were by and large habituated to "other direction," were unable to use their extended "free time" to create, invent, play on their own. Their need for "other direction" put a great deal of stress on parents. This, however, was not the case in all households.

In homes where children had greater inner resources, they were less likely to succumb to anxiety. They were less likely to depend on others to direct their home activities. They were more able to use their extended "free time" at home to find ways to engage, positively, in a variety of activities that benefited them in numerous ways.

In no other period of time was the difference between self-directed and outer-directed children more obvious. In no other period of time was that difference more relevant for the development of self-directed, "can-do" children.

The development and nurturance of can-do children begins in infancy and builds during toddler ages. It comes from giving children choices—providing them with the materials and the conditions in which they may engage on their own—within, of course, parameters of safety. It means respecting those choices. It comes from ensuring that they are safe, well nourished, secure, and loved unconditionally. It comes from providing them with the "toys" that engage them and getting out of their way as they engage. It comes from never doubting their efforts to "do" and from showing, with words and behavior, that you, the adult, have confidence in their ability to do.

As they are able to manage more independently, beginning with when they are able to walk and get around on their own, providing them with the toys and tools for their creative activities is one more building block for their empowerment. Building blocks such as Lego and Duplo can afford hours of creative building and inventing. As can washable paints, colored felt pens, crayons, and lots of colored and white paper; modeling clay, finger paint, dull-ended scissors; stuffed animals, toy cars and trucks, toy household utensils, like plates, knives, forks, measuring cups and spoons, pots, pans, eggbeaters; dress-up costumes with hats, masks, shoes and boots, handbags; puppets; jigsaw puzzles; mazes.

Of course, not all of these toys and tools are offered all at once, as that would likely be overwhelming and counterproductive. A small selection of toys and tools is a good beginning, and these options are changed and exchanged as interests shift.

If there's a garden, that would be the place for a larger water table or sand table. If not, big basins or plastic tubs, with the floor protected with plastic sheeting, are alternatives for investigations with floating and sinking things and measuring. Some children spend hours with Keva blocks, not only building structures but using them in more inventive ways, like forming letters and making doll furniture. Not to be neglected are paper, pencils, felt pens, and perhaps paper-bound journal books for writing stories and drawing.

And of course, children's books. Lots and lots of children's books.

For parents who are financially limited, secondhand stores for discarded and often nearly new children's toys and games are a wonderful resource. These thrift shops are often well supplied with children's toys, games, and books for a fraction of the cost of brand new ones.

When there is more than one child at home, two or more youngsters would certainly extend play opportunities, because, as five-year-old philosopher Eli reminded us, "It's always better with a friend."

If and when a parent wants to spend time with a child at play, it is important for that parent to remember not to take control over the play, not to tell the child what to do and how, not to intervene with "better" ideas. And never, never praising or rewarding what the child has done, because excessive praise for a child's creative work has the tendency to defeat all efforts to develop can-do children.

Allowing a child control over his or her play actions provides them with the skills they need to develop and nurture their own sense of inner-direction.

CONCLUSION

Providing young children with toys and tools that challenge their thinking, respecting them and their ideas, allowing them choices and respecting their decisions, and encouraging and validating their creative and investigative play are the essential conditions of empowerment and the nurturing and development of the self-directed, "can-do" child. Throughout the following chapters, suggestions are offered for how these ideas are put to work.

Fig. 4.1. Maya. Permission granted by Lin Snow

SECTION II
Classroom Applications

Chapter 5

Introduction to the Activities

The school is tucked out of sight on a cul-de-sac, hiding its advanced age and its shabby look from the mainstream downtown traffic. A relic of the time when the town was a small farming village, it now sits within a district populated by newly built tract homes and brand-new schools. While the new schools serve the newly arrived suburbanites, Roberts Elementary School enrolls children from a markedly different population: welfare families, single parents, and other groups who live in the downtown core.

The personal crises that occur each school day at Roberts exceed, by tenfold, what happens in any of the other schools in the district. The teachers at Roberts have more than their share of heartache over the lives and well-being of their students.

SCENES FROM A CLASSROOM

Lee Summers has been teaching for five years, but this is his first year using the Play-Debrief-Replay approach with his grade two class as a way of organizing instruction for his students (Wassermann and Ivany 2022).

The room is abuzz with child-directed activities. Five groups of children are working in investigative play centers with dry cells, buzzers, low-wattage light bulbs, and switches. They are carrying out their own investigations with these materials. Lee has used the following activity card to guide them:

> Use the materials in this center to find out what you can about electricity and how it works.
> - What can you observe about the dry cells? The buzzers? The light bulb?
> - Talk together about your observations and make some notes about what you did.

Lee observes the children in one of the "electricity" centers and sees that they are implicitly testing the idea that an increase in the number of dry cells strung together will increase the brightness of the light. They try increasing the number of batteries to three and the light brightens. A shout goes up from the investigators. They begin to rewire with four dry cells. By this time, their enthusiasm has attracted an audience of children from some of the other groups who have come over to observe. The four-cell hypothesis is supported, accompanied by shouts and laughter. "Try six," one observer suggests, while others go back to their play centers to test the same hypothesis.

Meanwhile, another group in the rear of the classroom is working with a buzzer, testing different ways of wiring and clamping. When the buzzer sounds, they laugh as if watching a clown fall off a stool.

No child is off task. They are either conducting investigations or observing others' inquiries. There is no behavior management necessary. Not once does the teacher have to intervene to tell a child to "settle down" or to "behave" or to "get to work." If there are arguments, they are more about what should be tried next. The teacher does not observe any interpersonal conflict. Even though it is almost time for recess, none of the children has lost interest in the investigations. When the recess bell sounds, the children respond in a wail.

"Oh, Mr. Summers, do we *have* to go outside today?"

Lee smiles and suggests that the children may choose to go or stay, and for those who wish to stay, he would remain in the classroom. Six children get their jackets and leave. The rest continue their investigative play.

While Lee is very much "present" in that classroom, he does not intervene to direct the children's investigations. He does not ever say, "Why don't you try it *that* way?" or, "Now do *this*!" His responses to the children are more reflective in nature. For example, "I see that you are now going to repeat the experiment with five dry cells." Or encouraging and supportive. For example, "Hah! I can see that you've got that working just as you thought it would."

A small girl named Nadya approaches Lee and asks, "Mr. Summers, where is the masking tape?"

He tells her that the last time he saw it, it was over on the shelf, but that she might have to look around, as other children were using it. Lee knows that Nadya is new to the class and that her behavior is less self-reliant than most of the other children who have, at this stage of the school year (February), grown considerably in their ability to "do" for themselves. But, Lee believes, given time in this program, she will become more independent and solve these and other kinds of problems on her own.

When the children return from recess, additional time is allocated to the investigative play with the notice that the teacher intends to "debrief" the play at eleven o'clock. Just before the hour, Lee calls for cleanup. The materials are packed away and stored for easy access for tomorrow's investigations, and the children gather in a large group at the front of the room. Lee begins the discussion with an invitation:

Teacher: Tell me about some of the observations you made as you investigated with your dry cells.

Frank: We were tryin' to see if the light would get brighter if we put more batteries on.

Teacher: You added more dry cells to see if that would make any difference.

Frank: Yeah.

Teacher: And what did you observe?

Kuldip: When we put four cells, the light got brighter. We was goin' to do it with six cells.

Teacher: You have a hypothesis about what might happen with six cells.

Kuldip: It would be very bright. Real bright.

(*Many kids nodding in agreement.*)

Teacher: The more cells, the brighter the light? Is that your theory?

Kuldip: Yup!

Teacher: I wonder how that happens. How do you explain it?

Sarah: Well, I think you got more power there. You see there's power in the cells. So if you have more cells, you got more power and that makes the light brighter.

Teacher: The dry cells have power. The more power, the brighter the light?

Sarah: Yeah.

Teacher: Thank you Sarah, for giving us your theory. Does anyone have any observations that would support Sarah's theory—the theory that dry cells have power and the more power you add, the more electrical energy you get?

Lee continues the debriefing in this fashion, calling for students' ideas, listening carefully to what each child is saying, reflecting the statements accurately, building their science vocabulary, and fleshing out important concepts. He does not judge any idea as right or wrong; neither does he praise ("That's a good idea!") or condemn ("No, that won't work"). He does not lead students to recite or provide certain pieces of information. Instead he respectfully hears, attends, and "plays back" the ideas presented, using students' statements as building blocks to help them reach for the deeper meanings, the "big ideas" underlying their investigations.

It is this process that ensures that each child feels listened to, respected, important. Every investigation, every idea, every child receives the same courtesy. Lee is likely, too, to raise at least one "puzzler"—a question that might spur new investigations when the children return to "replay" with the same materials in the following days. Some examples of those "puzzlers" are:

- In what ways are the electric light model and the buzzer model alike? How are they different? What theories do you have about that?
- Where do you suppose the "power" in the dry cell comes from? What are your thoughts on this?
- In what ways is the dry-cell-light-bulb model like the electric light system in the room? How is it different? What are your ideas about it?

In the days that follow, children "replay" with the same materials, carrying out new and more sophisticated investigations or replicating investigations already done. Variables are manipulated and results compared. In subsequent replays, Lee adds some new materials to the centers that present new options: simple electric motors, dead batteries, and different types of switches.

In this classroom Lee demonstrates how the conditions for growing self-directed, "can-do" children are met, through respect for children and their choices, active engagement in tasks that challenge thinking, and involvement in creative and investigative play.

PLAY-DEBRIEF-REPLAY: A WAY OF ORGANIZING FOR INSTRUCTION

The instructional framework called play-debrief-replay was not dreamed up in a university laboratory. It has been observed in dozens of classrooms in which teachers of all levels of instruction found ways to supply basic learning conditions that empower students and elevate their intelligent habits of mind (Wassermann and Ivany 2022). It is not the only curriculum framework in which children become empowered. However, providing opportunities for creative, investigative play, followed by helping children to reflect on their play experiences and then encouraging them to build on earlier experiences through replay, does what it claims.

Children who learn under these conditions are empowered. They learn intelligent habits of mind, and they become more self-initiating, responsible, creative, and inventive. They grow in their capacity to understand "big ideas" within the curriculum. Within their play, different learning styles, different learning tempos, and different talents are all naturally accommodated. Concepts are learned through hands-on, practical experience—the way learners at any age actually begin to understand.

Whether a child's preferred learning mode is spatial or linguistic (Gardner 1991), play-debrief-replay seems to provide the learning conditions that allow each one to accommodate to his or her individual learning needs. In Gardner's terms, "intuitive" learners and the "disciplined expert" rise easily to the challenges of independent inquiry, taking giant steps on the pathway of meaning making.

Those students whom Gardner terms "traditional"—those "lesson learners" who are primarily concerned with getting the right answers—are at first bewildered by the expectation that they function as independent, autonomous problem solvers. However, after several weeks of working under these conditions, even "traditional" students become more adventurous, more generative, more resourceful, more flexible.

With many years of implementation in classrooms, play-debrief-replay, perhaps under different labels, is found embedded in instruction in university-level courses, professional development programs, and elementary and secondary school classrooms. Student feedback from their experiences is enthusiastic: skill levels increase, students claim they feel respected, conceptual understanding grows. Adult learners are particularly eloquent in citing how learning under these conditions empowers them (Wassermann and Ivany 2022; Adam 1992; Ewing 1990).

The play-debrief-replay approach also provides teachers with a clearly articulated plan for moving teaching for thinking from the level of educational theory into classroom practice. That is,

- Play activities are interwoven with higher-order thinking, providing students with intellectual and creative challenges.
- Debriefing requires students to reflect on and to seek out conceptual meanings of substance.
- Replay promotes continued examination and reflection.

Programs in which children's participation in developing their own conceptual understandings by using their own ways of learning in a flexible environment have long been supported in the research of Piaget and Inhelder (1969). In more recent years, constructivist theory, a child-centered orientation to teaching and learning, has evolved from this earlier work. Based on the belief that learners actively create, interpret, and reorganize knowledge in individual ways (Windschitl 1999), constructivist classrooms operating at all instructional levels utilize pedagogies in which teachers, instead of pushing content at students, aim at eliciting in-depth understandings and appreciations.

The options for teachers who use a play-debrief-replay program are vast. The approach rests on respect for teachers as highly trained professionals. There are no formulas to be followed in rote application. Instead an organizational scheme is suggested that is played out according to teacher and student needs and curriculum concerns. The instructional stages may be clear, but much choice is left to the teacher with respect to the how and the what. It invites teachers to try, to experiment, to generate hypotheses to be tested in the real world of the classroom.

If children are empowered through these methods, so are teachers.

SERIOUS PLAYERS

Teachers who wish to teach children an important concept begin by designing a play experience. The play allows children to study the concept through active, investigative examination, as observed in Lee Summers's class, described at the beginning of this chapter. Play is generally carried out in cooperative learning groups, in which children contribute substantially to each other's investigations and creative endeavors. The teacher usually designs the play around a curriculum concept that is important for children to study and learn. The teacher also provides the play materials that allow for hands-on and "minds-on" investigations, organizes the learning groups, and sets the stage for the play to proceed.

The children are the players.

During play the teacher observes but does not participate or direct, unless specific behavior management is called for. This may be a new way of looking at the "act of teaching"—a departure from the "banking model" (Freire 1983; Wassermann 2021), in which the teacher tells, and therefore "deposits," information into the child's head. Rather, this is a "theatrical" model, in which the teacher writes the play, gathers the props, sets the stage, and once the play has begun, assumes the role of stage manager. Stage managers see to it that the play goes on. (Directors, on the other hand, tell the players what to do and how.)

As there are plays like *Macbeth* and other plays like *A Lie of the Mind*, so are there differences between the kinds of play opportunities that teachers may design for children. The richer the play, the more potential it has for concept development, creativity, and the examination of issues of substance. A play calling for observation of a button may not be worth the price of admission. While a play involving observations of many kinds of leaves may lead to substantive and far-reaching understandings in the field of botany.

Productive play activities that yield significant conceptual growth share several criteria:

1. They are open-ended. They do not lead students to "the answers."
2. They call for the generation of ideas, rather than the recall of specific pieces of information.
3. They challenge student thinking; in fact, they require thinking. Higher-order mental challenges are built into each play task.
4. They are messy. Children are playing around; stuff falls on the floor and hands get dirty.
5. Learning through play is nonlinear, nonsequential.
6. They focus on the "big ideas"—those important concepts of the curriculum—rather than on small details.
7. They provide opportunities for children to grow in their conceptual understanding. When children carry out investigations, they grow in their ability to understand important meanings.
8. The children are the players. They are actively involved in learning, talking to each other, sharing ideas, laughing, and getting excited about what they have found. They are not sitting quietly, passively listening to the teacher's thinking.
9. Children are working together, in cooperative learning groups. Their play is enhanced through their collaborative investigations. Cooperation rather than competition is stressed.

SOME CAVEATS

When children are only just beginning to work in groups and, for the first time, being asked to take the initiative rather than just follow orders, they are likely to benefit more from play activities that allow for fewer options. After they have developed more ability to choose and more confidence as creators, as they become more "self-directed," play tasks that are more open-ended may be added. The teacher is the one who appraises the situation and makes that judgment.

Investigative play activities become the way of teaching curriculum content. They are not "extras" or enrichment activities outside the "real work" of the curriculum. Play is the vehicle through which curriculum content is intelligently and thoughtfully learned, and because the play always involves challenges to pupil thinking, thinking becomes the method of learning.

In the primary grades, play can and should also include traditional creative/imaginative activities using sand and water tables, clay, blocks, Lego or other constructions, paint, "Wendy houses," arts and crafts, scissors and paste, music, songs, and dance. It can and should occur as well in language learning, the learning of numbering and measuring, and learning about the world in which we live through sociological and scientific inquiries. Numerous examples of investigative play activities in the creative and content areas are found in subsequent chapters of this book.

Designing a play experience requires teachers' awareness of how concepts are taught through pupils' active engagement with selected materials and how higher-order thinking skills are incorporated into the play task. Play activities also reflect the substantive issues of the curriculum—that is, what the teacher thinks important for the children to learn. Teachers who design play experiences for children in this "theatrical" model of instruction challenge themselves consistently to provide the richest learning opportunities for children. Perhaps that is why teachers who use this approach feel exhilarated, energized, and empowered in the process.

DEBRIEFING: USING PLAY TO PROMOTE REFLECTION

Experiential play provides introductory learning opportunities during which children carry out explorations, investigations, and dramatic scenarios with the materials that are provided. When the play period is over (the time allotted for play will vary), the teacher uses the play experience as a basis for promoting reflection and increasing children's understanding of the "big ideas." This reflection-on-action stage has been labeled "debriefing," and chapter 6 has been devoted to this procedure.

It is during debriefing that the teacher assumes an active role. This discussion uses provocative questioning and facilitative responding to enable children to make sense of discrepancies, shed naïve theories for more mature and informed ones, and take the next steps toward new insights and understandings. Ramsey (1998) writes that to "raise children as critical thinkers, we do not want them to remain in a comfortable state of equilibrium. Instead we want them to learn to continuously question and challenge their information and assumptions about the status quo."

In the play-debrief-replay model of instruction, children learn not only to live with uncertainty, but to embrace it.

During debriefing, the teacher calls the group together to discuss aspects of their play. Debriefing may be carried out with the whole class or with smaller groups, depending on which organization is more suited to the teacher's or group's needs. Whatever the size of the group, the teacher uses reflective questioning strategies (seen in the Lee Summers example above). While many examples of debriefing dialogues are presented in chapter 6 and sample debriefing questions are included for each investigative play in the activities chapters, some examples are provided here.

If children have been engaged in play, the teacher might ask,

- What observations have you made?
- How did you know that was true?
- How did you figure it out?
- How did get that to work? Can you explain it?

If the play has been with materials of construction, the teacher might ask,

- Tell me about what you have built.
- How did that work?
- What did you do to make it work?
- What was that good for?
- Do you have any other ideas for building?

If the play has been dramatic, the teacher might ask,

- Tell me about the play.
- What were the parts you liked best?
- What were some funny (or sad) parts?

If the play was physical-motor, the teacher might ask,

- Tell me about your activities.
- What was hard for you to do? What was easy?
- What do you like best about it?

If the play was with games, the teacher might ask,

- Tell me about your games.
- What did you like about them?
- What problems did you have? How did you work them out?

These reflective questioning strategies accomplish many things. In the first instance, they require children to reflect on their experiences, and they call for higher-order cognitive processing. Because the children are asked to respond, they must cognitively frame what they have done and articulate the experience through oral language. It is a process of extracting the big ideas, the essential meanings, from their play experiences.

Another condition of debriefing is that children refine their language skills in communicating their ideas. Through these discussions, they are called on to articulate, to give voice to, their cognitive experiences. In all of these interactions, higher-order thinking and language development are being engaged and practiced.

It is obvious that such discussion strategies empower children as thinkers. They call for children's assuming responsibility for reporting on and comprehending what they have done. They are also respectful, for they ask children to tell about their own experiences. They invite children's ideas, and their ideas are listened to and given serious consideration. Such questioning strategies are often called "facilitative." The respect that they convey builds children's esteem and empowers them cognitively.

Debriefing, effectively done, lays the groundwork for carrying out the subsequent play. Later play experiences evolve from the kinds of questions that teachers raise, leading to potential new plays and investigations. Replay forms the third leg of the instructional plan, as children continue to construct knowledge and make sense of the world.

REPLAY: RETURNING TO THE SCENE OF THE INVESTIGATION

Replay follows debriefing and generally occurs over the next few days. It may involve repetition of the investigation, and many young children enjoy and benefit from this, especially when it is their own choice. Replay may involve the addition of new materials, to give children's inquiries a new focus. It may move the investigations into another, related area of the curriculum.

Replay has several purposes. It provides additional practice with the concepts and skills. Investigations may be replicated, findings verified, and new variables manipulated. The inquiry may be extended into new, related areas, taking the concepts several steps further. More sophisticated, challenging investigations may be called for, based on concepts developed in earlier plays.

Replay may also show how relationships exist among the disciplines. It builds on previous experience and thus amplifies and provides development of understandings. Its spiraling path allows children to return to play with the concepts at subsequent levels of development. It allows for children to look at experience in retrospect, leaving open the possibility that some point not grasped initially will become simplified when tackled at a later play stage.

The play-debrief-replay process with developing concepts may carry on for as long as the teacher perceives there is benefit to the experience. It is likely that play will continue to be generative and that only pressures of time and the need to move on to other important studies will be the reasons for terminating the cycle. Never mind. There are lots of play opportunities and lots of exciting new concepts to play with.

AT HOME

If such teaching and learning strategies are effective in classrooms, how might parents implement such procedures with young children at home?

Not to make a situation too arduous for parents, some suggestions are offered in this section to show how the curriculum framework may be implemented at home. Once again, the significant conditions are these: allowing and respecting children's choices; providing hands-on materials to use for concept development; offering a variety of enrichment materials; maintaining a hands-off policy while children play; and following up the play with a discussion that allows children to present their ideas in the presence of reflective and nonjudgmental questions and responses.

It will be obvious, at first glance, that the play activities suggested below do not include any of the "screen time" activities available on tablets, computers, or iPhones. The reasons for this come from the most recent research about the downsides of too much time spent on video games and tablets.

According to reports from the National Library of Medicine, too much screen time is more than likely to contribute to difficulties with sleep, attention deficit problems, anxiety, and even obesity. Sitting and watching a screen or playing video games is time that is not spent being physically active—one of the most important elements in the healthful growth and development of young children. For these reasons, screen time is noticeably absent from the list of play activities below.

To offer children choices about their play activities, some parents have found a "choosing board" to be a helpful tool. A large piece of poster board, divided in sections, provides the necessary information. The column to the left lists the play options. The list is generated by children working with a parent in creating the options. There are small push pins available and several disks, each with a child's name. At the beginning of "choosing time," a child picks up the disk with his or her name and places it alongside the activity that he or she has chosen for the play session.

Of course, parents will need to ensure that the relevant materials are available for the play centers. Keeping a supply of materials stored and readily available makes the setting up of centers easier.

As children choose, they take the disk with their name and hang it on the hook next to the center of their choice. Depending on the allowed time for play, children may play at one center or perhaps two.

Creating a choosing board may be overegging the pudding. Children may, of course, simply tell a parent what they would like to do during their play time. This is a lot less cumbersome and a more informal way of making choices. However, what it lacks is the visual "record" of play activities that the choosing board makes obvious. In the end, parents will choose the strategies that are more consistent with their own aims and goals for their young children at play.

Play time is then followed by a home version of debriefing. It may look and sound like this:

Parent: Tell me about your choice of play activity today.

Mila: I choose the Keva blocks.

Parent: I noticed that you chose Keva blocks yesterday as well. You seem to enjoy playing with Keva blocks very much.

Mila: I like the way you can build anything with them.

Parent: You can build lots of different things. Tell me about some of the things you built.

Mila: Well, first I built a tower. I wanted to see how tall I could make it.

Parent: And how did that work out for you?

Mila: I had to stand on a chair and I made it very tall.

Parent: Did you have any trouble with the building of your tower?

Mila: Well, I couldn't reach the top. I had to stand on a chair.

Parent: How did you make sure the tower didn't fall down? What ideas did you have about doing that?

Mila: I tried it before and it did fall down. I think it is because the blocks weren't even. You have to make them even so they won't fall down.

Parent: There's something about making sure the blocks are even in the building of the tower. So it won't fall down.

Mila: Yeah. Mine didn't fall this time. It was straight. Now I can knock it down and that's fun too.

Parent: Building is fun but knocking the building down is also fun. Do you think you will choose Keva blocks again tomorrow?

Mila: Yeah. I want to build something else.

Parent: Do you have any ideas about it?

Mila: I don't know yet. I have to see how I feel.

Parent: Okay. Let's get the materials cleaned up for today so they will be ready for tomorrow's play.

Lin Snow often uses investigative play in providing opportunities for her two children to experiment, discover, and become immersed in extending their knowledge and skills with home activities. She had some jars of no longer fresh spices to create materials for Kai and his friend Wade to play with:

> I've been cleaning out our spice drawer in the kitchen and had about a dozen old jars that I was going to throw away. Kai was waiting for his friend Wade to come for playdate. And while he was waiting I gave him a bowl and some measuring spoons with free reign over the discarded spices. When Wade arrived, Kai took him over and showed him how to mix spices. The two of them played for a long time with those spices. Some of my favorite comments overheard were:
> - *Pass me that red one. Paprika! Weird word.*
> - *I know that's cinnamon you opened because I can smell it already.*
> - *Mine is white now because I put cream of tartar in.*
> - *Wait! Your spoon is different than mine. I have one teaspoon and yours says 'one-half' and it's smaller.*
> - *What happens if we add water?*
> - *This says cloves but smells like cinnamon too.*

My parent/teacher heart was soaring! Especially since these kids act so cool a lot of the time. They eventually got tired of spices and wandered off. But later they came back to the spice table, sitting there for almost an hour, mixing, stirring, smelling. To think I nearly tossed those jars into the trash! The kids were also very sweet about cleaning up afterwards, probably because it was such fun. I asked if I should toss the spices away and got a very emphatic, "*No!* We want to play after school tomorrow!"

BUT DOES IT WORK?

Will this way of learning through play and, through it, the development of personal power, self-respect, intelligent habits of mind, and inner-direction be sufficient to ensure the growth outcomes that teachers and parents consider essential in the education of young children? It may not be everything that we as teachers (and parents) should do, but the data so far suggest that such conditions do, in fact, contribute substantially to fostering these important learning outcomes. But how will we know?

The behavior of the children will be the telling point. If we are using teaching strategies that are not effective in delivering the learning goals we consider essential, or if we see children's behavior deteriorating rather than improving, then it may well be that what we are doing needs serious rethinking.

If, on the other hand, the way we have organized the curriculum and the teaching strategies we have employed have led to growth in those behaviors we value (increased personal power, a sense of can-do, growing self-respect, responsible individual and group behavior, problem-solving skills, inner direction), then we may take heart that what we are doing is, in fact, working.

In the chapters that follow, more explicit help is provided in translating the ideas in these introductory chapters into classroom practice. By making teaching strategies specific and concrete, teachers will more easily bridge the gap between these ideas and the day-to-day life of the classroom, ensuring success for every teacher.

Chapter 6

Debriefing

Using Interactions That Promote Reflection

Teachers and parents interact with children hundreds of times each day, choosing from an extensive repertoire of possible responses that attend to specific concerns, to particular events, to organizational and management matters, to children's ideas, to behavior. These responses are often formulated quickly, within the give and take of an extended discussion. This interactive process, intense and demanding, asks a lot of teachers and parents: to respond thoughtfully, appropriately and sensitively, in ways that are helpful and not hurtful, when the environment is charged with energy and other stressful demands.

It is no wonder that teachers and parents feel exhausted at the end of each day. The interactive process of responding to children demands great thoughtfulness, sensitivity, and a high level of professional functioning. It is not only a matter of responding; it is also determining which response is the most appropriate for a given situation. For example:

> Some responses give information: *You'll find help with those questions on page 11 of your textbook.*
>
> Some give examples: *Here, I'll show you how to do that long division.*
>
> Some are directive: *Sean, please clean up your room! It's a mess!*
>
> Some are judgmental: *I think your artwork is wonderful! You have such a great sense of color and design.*
>
> Some are empathic: *I can see how angry you are because the other kids didn't want you on the team.*

Other responses require children to think about issues, ideas, and concepts, calling for reflection, for deeper understanding, for making meaning of the "big ideas." They may also invite children to come up with new ideas. For example:

- *Tell me a little more about what you observed.*
- *When you put that heavy piece of wood into the water, you expected that it would sink. You were surprised that it floated! I wonder how you could explain that?*
- *When Ian measured it, he found that it was thirteen centimeters wide. When Sarah measured it, she found it was fourteen centimeters wide. How do you explain that, I wonder?*
- *You say that lemons are exactly like eggs. I wonder if you can find any differences between them?*
- *Which one would you choose? How did you make that choice?*
- *Which would be the better way to go? What are your ideas about it?*

How do teachers and parents learn the interactive skills that promote reflection and foster children's independence? How do they learn to choose appropriate responses, monitoring what they say and watching for the effect of their responses on the child? How do teachers and parents learn to use interactions that promote intelligent habits of mind and a can-do ethos?

LEARNING THE INTERACTION SKILLS FOR DEBRIEFING

A beginner practicing her golf swing is told, "It's all in the wrist!" A newcomer to debriefing is told, "It's all in attending." While both are overstatements, both point out important clues to skill development.

Successful interactions begin with mastering the skill of attending, a simple but vastly neglected tool in human conversations. Attending means listening very closely to what the other person is saying. It means "clearing your ears and your head" of extraneous "noise" (your own intruding thoughts) so that you may "tune in" to exactly what is being said.

Attending involves more than just listening. It involves the ability to hear not only the words but the nuances of expression, to discern deeper and unstated meanings. It involves picking up on the affect, so that the statement is heard in context. It means hearing and comprehending the "fullness" of what is being said and freeing oneself from the desire to comment on or judge it (Carkhuff 1969). In these days when adults who care for children are frequently overworked and overextended, it is no small feat to stop and give a child the full attention that attending to their statements demands. But without that, all is lost.

The first steps in mastering the skill of attending involve the following:

1. Making and holding eye contact with the speaker.
2. Listening to what is being said. Being naturally interested. Showing in your body language that you care about what the speaker is saying.
3. Discerning the tone, the nuances of expression.
4. Looking for evidence of affect (verbal or nonverbal) that the speaker is revealing.
5. Being aware of indicators of stress shown by the speaker.
6. Avoiding commenting on the speaker's idea.
7. Avoiding giving your own idea in response to what the speaker is saying.
8. Taking in the full meaning of what is being said. Friere (1983) refers to this as "apprehending."
9. Making it safe for the speaker to present his or her ideas.

As you engage in all of these actions, you will come to a fuller apprehension of the child's statement. You will be able to take in the deeper meanings of what is being said. While you are in the process of doing all of that, begin to think about formulating a response that

- Does not judge the child's idea, in either tone or word
- Thoughtfully and accurately paraphrases or "says back in a new way" the child's idea
- Is respectful; shows natural interest; helps the speaker to feel safe, nondefensive, nonthreatened

As you respond, observe the effect of what you said on the speaker. Especially watch the eyes to discern how your response has been "received"—whether it helps the child to use your response productively, or if it has caused stress and a defensive reaction.

It's funny that "attending behaviors" should require so much concentrated effort. We all perceive ourselves to be very good listeners, when in fact we are so busy trying to get our own ideas out that we rarely pay heed to what the other person is saying. This is especially true when we interact with young children, since very few of us take the time to listen fully and appreciate their ideas, so preoccupied are we in trying to give them the benefit of our own wisdom.

RESPONSES THAT PARAPHRASE

If you are just beginning to refine your skills in responding in ways that encourage children's thoughtfulness, begin with learning about responses that paraphrase a child's ideas. There are several reasons why this makes sense.

First, the paraphrase response is the most natural to master. It is not something that has to be struggled with. It is formulated from the child's statement. Second, it allows you to concentrate on your attending skills at the same time. Third, it sets the debriefing interactions in motion. You can practice attending, pacing, paraphrasing, and reflecting on the effect of your response, all the while engaging in productive debriefing. Fourth, while paraphrasing may appear to be less fruitful, that is far from the truth. These responses do, in fact, require a child to think more about what he or she has said. Used effectively, they are enormously productive in encouraging and extending a child's intelligent habits of mind.

When a parent or teacher sets out to truly listen, to apprehend, to attend to what a child is saying, and then uses those ideas to feed back to him or her, it may be the very first time that child has the experience of being truly listened to. It may be the first time that the child realizes that someone important is actually listening to what is coming out of their mouth. It may be the first time that the child hears their words played back—"mirrored" for them to hear in a new construction.

This is a powerful tool in the child's realization that he or she must take responsibility for formulating ideas intelligently. Someone is actually listening!

A paraphrase can be a straightforward "saying back" in different words:

Child: Sometimes you find sharks in the deep parts of the ocean.

Adult: Sharks live in the deeper waters of the ocean.

A paraphrase can interpret what the child has said by "reading into" the statement:

Child: Sometimes you find sharks in the deep parts of the ocean.

Adult: So sharks are not likely to be found in the shallow parts. Only in the deeper parts.

A paraphrase can interpret, as well as "read in" affect:

Child: Sometimes you find sharks in the deep parts of the ocean.

Adult: So it might be safer to swim in shallower water and more dangerous to swim in the deep parts.

A debriefing session in which a child's ideas are carefully and thoughtfully reflected in paraphrased responses can work effectively to illuminate the big ideas in any area of inquiry. Here's an example of how this works:

The teacher in the example below is focusing the discussion on different approaches to mask making. The "big ideas" underlying the discussion are the ways different media are used to create works of art and that masks are used in different cultures for different purposes.

Teacher: You have had a chance to work together in your groups to compare and discuss these two masks. What observations have you made about how they are alike and how they are different?

Tanya: They both have big noses.

Teacher: The noses are something you noticed first.

Kirsten: They both have their mouths open.

Teacher: Open mouths. That's another feature you noticed.

Brian: They're both Indian masks.

Teacher: There's something about the masks that tells you they have been made by Indians.

Brian: Yeah. I think that Indians wear masks.

Teacher: Indians use masks. I guess they couldn't be Japanese. Is that what you mean?

Brian: No. They look like Indian masks to me. *(He begins to be a little unsure, looks at masks again and maybe is examining his assumption.)*

Sam: I could see that they are made of different material. They both look like they're made of wood, but they're not. This one is wood *(knocks on it)* but this one is something else.

Teacher: This one is wood. You seem pretty certain of that. And this one is some other material. You're not sure.

Sam: I don't know. It's too light for wood. *(Continues to finger as he observes the papier-mâché mask.)*

Arlyn: It could be light wood. I saw some light wood. It hardly weighs anything.

Teacher: Maybe it's a very lightweight wood.

Sam: I don't think so. Look at this. It's like a little piece of paper is pulling off this edge. *(He peers at a place where the paper is beginning to pull away.)*

Teacher: You think this mask might be made of paper.

Sam: But it can't be paper, unless it's a very thick paper. Otherwise the paper would tear. It's too hard for just plain paper.

Teacher: If it's paper it's got to be very thick paper. Otherwise, it couldn't last very long.

Sam: Yeah. *(He's thinking about it.)*

Teacher: You want to think about it some more?

Sam: Yeah.

Using only paraphrasing in her responses, the teacher skillfully opens out the children's observations and comparisons in an examination of the use of mask-making media. She does this without inserting any of her own ideas or judging the quality of their ideas. She does this without raising "why" questions that challenge children's thinking prematurely, before they have had a chance to examine and compare data. As Sherlock Holmes reminded us, "It's impossible to theorize in the absence of data."

In fact, the "big ideas" of a debriefing guide the teacher's use of paraphrasing, and the art lies in bringing these big ideas under examination without telling, directing, or judging. The skills for doing this grow over time as teachers and parents open themselves to repeated and long-term self-scrutiny of their debriefing interactions—in other words, learning to hear ourselves as we speak.

More sophisticated responses, both from the adult's perspective of formulating them and from the children's perspective of having to respond, include those that require the making of analyses and the generation of new ideas. Both of these kinds of responses are used much more sparingly than paraphrasing and they are interspersed in and among paraphrasing, as appropriate.

RESPONSES THAT CALL FOR ANALYSIS

Responses that require children to make analyses ask them to reflect more deeply and beyond their firsthand observations. These responses include asking that examples be given, asking if assumptions are being made, asking where the idea came from, asking if the child has thought about alternatives, asking that comparisons be made, and asking for data to support the idea.

This does not exhaust the list of possible responses that call for analysis. There are others that may be particularly appropriate in responding to a child's idea. There is also a hierarchy within this category—that is, some responses are more demanding than others. Difficulty and challenge are likely to vary from situation to situation, from child to child. The happy news is that, as children get more experience with being responded to in these ways, they learn habits of thinking. That is, when at first a child may blanch upon being asked for an example, in later sessions, after extended experience with developing habits of thinking, examples are likely to come more easily.

This, of course, is the great reward of teaching-for-thinking interactions. Children learn habits of thinking. They learn to take more responsibility for what they say, to base arguments on data, to examine alternatives before choosing, and to think about ideas rather than merely collecting bytes of information. These habits of thinking do not appear after one, two, or three play-debrief sessions, but the data are clear that they do appear, over time, in the presence of such teaching-for-thinking classroom practices (Wassermann and Ivany 2022).

Responses that call for analysis include:

- Asking for an example: *Can you give me an example of how that works?*
- Asking for any assumptions that have been made: *I'm wondering if you've made an assumption here.*
- Asking why the child thinks this is good: *You seem to like that a lot. Am I wrong about that?*
- Asking if alternatives have been considered: *I'm wondering if you thought about any alternatives to that method?*
- Asking that comparisons be made: *How are those similar? How are they different?*
- Asking that data be classified: *How might you go about grouping them?*
- Asking what data support the idea: *You might have some data that back up your idea.*

The transcript below shows how responses calling for analysis are interspersed with basic paraphrasing responses. These are nine-year-old children, and their teacher is conducting a debriefing session following small-group discussions about a film shown in class about the importance of water in our lives.

Teacher: Tell me about some of your discussions about the ocean.

Margo: It's salty.

Teacher: The ocean is made of salt water. *(Paraphrases)* How did you discover that? *(Calls for analysis: Where did that idea come from?)*

Margo: When I went swimming, I got some in my mouth and it tasted very salty. Ugh.

Teacher: Tasting the water would be one way of telling that it was salty. *(Paraphrases)*

Margo: Yeah.

Teacher: I see. *(Accepts student's idea nonjudgmentally)* Thanks, Margo. *(Appreciates student's idea)* Are there other things that you can tell me about the water in the ocean? *(Returns to the initial question; therefore, it is not a response)*

Jason: Well, sometimes the water is very rough. If it is stormy, boats can sink.

Teacher: Ocean water can be rough. *(Paraphrases)* You're also telling us that the ocean can be used for boat travel. *(Paraphrases, by reading into the student's statement)*

Jason: Yeah. For boats, and seaplanes can land on it too.

Teacher: For boats and seaplanes. Different vehicles can travel on it. *(Paraphrases)* I see. *(Accepts student's idea)* Any other ideas about ocean water? *(Returns to the original question)*

Nicole: There are parts that are very deep. Very deep. Sometimes you can find sharks in the deep part.

Teacher: You are saying, Nicole, that sharks may live in the deep part of the ocean. *(Paraphrases)*

Nicole: Yup.

Teacher: How would you know that? *(Asks that an analysis be made: What data support the idea?)*

Nicole: I saw it on television.

Teacher: The television program helped you to know about the sharks that live in the ocean. *(Paraphrases)*

Billy: Other fish live in the ocean too, you know.

Teacher: The ocean's a place where other fish live as well. *(Paraphrases)*

Billy: Yeah. Salmon and whales. My father caught a salmon when he went fishing.

Teacher: *(Does not work with the idea that Billy's dad caught fish, although she does not reject it. She focuses instead on the bigger idea of marine life.)* You are telling me that many different kinds of fish live in the ocean. *(Paraphrases)*

(Children nod.)

Teacher: So let's see if I've got your ideas now. The ocean is used for travel. We swim in it. Fish—lots of different fish—live in the ocean. I wonder, what else is it good for? Any ideas? *(Asks that analyses be made: Why is this good?)*

As can be seen in the example above, responses that call for analysis demand more, cognitively, from children's thinking. Even more challenging are responses that call for the generation of new ideas.

RESPONSES THAT CHALLENGE

Responses that challenge thinking—the most difficult level—are those that call for the generation of new ideas. These ask children to extend their thinking beyond their firsthand observations into new and uncharted territory. These responses put students' thinking at the highest cognitive risk. They are used very sparingly during debriefing, interspersed appropriately within the basic paraphrase response patterns. These challenging responses include asking children to

- Generate hypotheses
- Interpret data
- Identify criteria used in making judgments
- Apply principles to new situations
- Make predictions about what is theoretically possible
- Explain how a theory might be tested
- Create new and imaginative schemes

Once again, these examples do not include all questions that challenge. However, they give an idea of the kinds of questions that constitute such challenges to children's thinking. They also demonstrate the complexity of what is being asked.

There are important caveats to the use of challenging questions. Not the least is that they should be used very selectively, perhaps never more than one or two in a short discussion. Challenging questions, by their very nature, shift the focus of the discourse into new areas. That is why too many challenging questions, asked in succession, give the discussion a jerky and erratic flow, jumping from one idea to another. It is the paraphrase that grounds the inquiry, allowing for a slower, more studied examination.

Since challenging questions are cognitively complex and require more sophisticated data processing, if they are used too soon in the discussion, they tend to stump children, especially those who are new to thinking about complex issues. They may frustrate them more than enable them. While some teachers may wish to believe that the greater challenge the better, long-term experiences with these discussions suggest otherwise.

The first-grade teacher in the following transcript is conducting a debriefing session following the children's play with the concepts of volume and capacity.

Teacher: Tell me about some of the other observations you made as you played with water and these different containers.

Peter: The tall one held the biggest water.

Teacher: You observed that the tall container held the most water. *(Paraphrases; uses her own adult vocabulary to inform Peter, without directly correcting his statement)*

(Several children nod in response to teacher's statement)

Teacher: So the tall container held more than any other container. *(Paraphrases by interpreting the intent of the statement)*

(Children nod in response)

Teacher: Tell me how you figured that out? *(Asks for analysis: What data support that idea?)*

Chi Chi: I could see how much there was in there.

Teacher: You could use your own eyes and you could see how much there was. Your eyes told you that the big, tall container held more water. *(Paraphrases and interprets)*

Chi Chi: Yup. *(Opens her eyes wide and ogles them)*

Teacher: *(Laughs)* That's one way of figuring it out! *(Accepts Chi Chi's strategy for making the determination)* I wonder if there are other ways? *(Not looking for the one "right" answer but for an examination of several ways determinations may be made)*

Aiden: Here's what I could do. I could fill up the tall container. Then I could pour it into this other big one here. Then I could see if there was any left over, or if it was the same.

Teacher: So you would check it out by comparing. You'd see if this short, fat container could hold as much water as the big, tall one, by pouring the water in and seeing if it held the same or not. *(Paraphrases)*

Aiden: Yup! That's what I did too.

Teacher: And what did you observe? *(Tell me more)*

Aiden: The same. It was the same for both.

Teacher: They both held the same amount, even though the big, tall one looked like it held more. *(Paraphrases and interprets)*

Aiden: *(Nods in assent)*

Teacher: Aiden disagrees with Peter and Chi Chi. Well, what do we do now? How can we know who to believe? *(Asks that analyses be made by asking for corroborating data to support these two different ideas)*

Deidre: We can do what Aiden says. Pour it in and see. Then we can know it.

Teacher: So do the same as Aiden did? Then we will know? *(Paraphrases)* But wait a second. Chi Chi says, "Our eyes tell us that the big, tall container holds more." Do your eyes tell you something that's wrong? *(Challenges: Asks students to apply principles to new situations)*

(Students get quiet. Teacher waits.)

Arlyn: *(Tentatively)* Sometimes we can't believe our eyes.

Teacher: Tell me more about that, Arlyn. *(Asks for more)*

Arlyn: When we think we see something and it's not really there.

Teacher: Our eyes can play tricks on us? *(Paraphrases)*

(Several children want to get in on this discussion.)

Ricky: You think you see it. You think it's small. But it's not.

Teacher: How does that work, Ricky? *(Asks that analyses be made; asks for an example)*

Ricky: Like in a car. When you first see it, it looks so small, puny like. Then you come close, and wow! It's this big giant thing.

Teacher: So if you are far away, something that is really large can look quite small. *(Paraphrases)*

Ricky: Yup.

(The other children nod.)

Teacher: I wonder how this applies to this container? *(Challenges: Asks that principles be applied to a new situation)*

Chi Chi: It could look bigger with your eyes, but maybe it's not as big as it looks.

In this transcript the teacher works with the children to examine the principle of conservation—the big idea that the space remains unchanged despite the rearrangement of the parts or the shape. Note particularly how the paraphrase response is used to help the children examine the observable data and how paraphrasing allows students to examine and reflect on their statements.

Note how "softly" the calls for analysis and challenges are worded, the points at which they are introduced, and how the examination of observable data leads naturally to the next steps of analysis and challenge. Note too how artfully the teacher uses paraphrasing, analysis, and challenging responses to help students in the examination of the big ideas.

THE ART OF RESPONDING NATURALLY

Having learned the skills of attending and paraphrasing, having recognized the nature of questions that call for analysis and the generation of new ideas, and having understood how all these pieces fit together is the equivalent of learning all the vocabulary words and phrases of a foreign language. With knowledge of words and phrases, the art of speaking in that foreign language in a way that can be understood calls for putting those words and phrases into sentences that communicate one's thoughts. Experience in using the language results, of course, in greater fluency.

This is also true of learning the skills of debriefing. Fluency comes after many, many sessions of using these discussion skills and learning to listen to yourself talk to children. Practice in this process is very much helped if you use a voice recorder available on most cell phones to record your discussions and listen to how the discussion proceeded. This allows you to study your interactive style, to be cognizant of your strengths, and to identify areas of needed growth. Unfortunately, there are no shortcuts to mastering the art of discussion skills, as there are no shortcuts to learning a new language.

In observing and monitoring your professional growth in the use of these discussion skills, try to remember these very important pieces of advice:

- Allow yourself adequate "growth time" in developing your skills. It's impossible to learn to speak French in a day or even a week. Have realistic expectations about your skill development.
- Practice, practice, practice, and continue your self-scrutiny as a discussion leader. Discussion skills do not grow via spontaneous generation but through the hard work of practice and reflection on practice.
- Instead of dwelling on your shortcomings, appreciate your successes.
- Pace yourself by attempting only as much as you feel you can handle. Never undertake so much that you are going to feel overwhelmed.

And finally, remember Paul Winchell's (1954) advice to aspiring ventriloquists: Don't rush. Don't get impatient. Don't get discouraged. Don't ever give up.

Chapter 7

Serious Players

The Arts

This chapter offers many suggestions for how creative, inventive, and unstructured play may be incorporated into the several areas of fine and performing arts: drama, arts and crafts, music, and the culinary arts! The suggestions are not exhaustive but may encourage teachers and parents who are eager to extend children's thinking about and engagement in these rich and creative areas.

DRAMATIC PLAY

Opportunities to dramatize, either purely inventive scenarios or those stories read and loved by children everywhere, should be a part of the daily life of children, either in school or at home. Dramatic play is greatly enhanced by props: dress-up clothes, hats, shoes, capes, gloves, wigs, crowns, swords, magic wands, kerchiefs, and scarves. More recent additions to such collections include plastic ornamental elf or rabbit ears, animal noses, deer horns and antlers, mustaches—all of which add to the fun of creative dramatic play.

In spontaneous dramatic play, no initial preparation is given. The children invent as they go along. Other, more structured dramas may be encouraged as well, but not one at the expense of another. For example, the acting out of a much loved story may begin with careful attention to the details of the story but evolve into an entirely new script.

Musical instruments may be added to introduce the idea of "musical theater." Classical music on CDs or audio files may also serve as background to the dramas. A raised platform or even some wooden boxes pushed together to serve as a stage, a curtain, or a puppet theater with hand puppets all add richness as well as inventiveness to the plays.

ARTS AND CRAFTS

Arts and crafts also represent an important dimension of what is essential in the creative life of children, young and older, more so today than ever, given the time that even young children now spend on their tablets. Opportunities abound, and many wonderful resources exist that add to the repertoire in the list below. In early childhood classrooms, these ideas may be carried out in "play centers," easily integrated into the primary curriculum. They also may be carried out at home. What is suggested here only scratches the surface of what can be done in these developmental years with arts and crafts materials.

- Painting with water colors, pastels, finger paint, poster paint
- Drawing and coloring with crayons, felt-tip pens, soft pencils, charcoal, colored chalk
- Cutting and pasting—making colored-paper collages, paper sculptures, mobiles
- Printing with linoleum blocks; hands, fingers, and commercially available stamps
- Mask making
- Weaving with paper strips, yarn
- Sculpting with clay, soap, scraps of wood, paper (origami)
- Building with wood and tools, blocks, Lego, Keva planks
- Puppet making with paper and cloth, paper bags
- Gluing mosaics of seeds, stones, pasta
- Sewing and knitting

Especially helpful is the series *Art in Action* by Guy Hubbard (1987), which contains dozens of inventive art projects for children and makes a close connection between creative art and thinking. Now out of print, copies are still available online from used book sellers.

MUSICAL PLAY

One reason teachers and parents stay at arm's length from including music in their classrooms or homes is their own perceived lack of musical background. Another is that, with music, there is noise, not an altogether welcome condition in the classroom or in an enclosed space at home. If noise is a problem for a teacher or parent, musical activities may fall to the bottom of the list of creative plays.

Serious Players 55

Fig. 7.1. Kai finger paints. Permission granted by Lin Snow

However, if a parent or teacher can draw on some musical experience in their background, what can be created for young children is both imaginative and rich. Even a musical virgin can inspire children to create, invent, and experience pleasure from making music.

Music "centers" can be created that involve experiences with listening, singing along, movement, and dancing. These may involve making and playing handmade instruments or playing with commercially available ones. They may include experimentation with sound and pitch, rhythm and beat, and melody.

1. *Listening and singing along.* Materials such as CDs and audio files, earbuds, and headphones may be included in this center. The music can include children's songs and sung stories, as well as selections from the classics and from musical theater.
2. *Listening, singing, movement, and dancing.* CDs and audio files are the primary tools in this center. Add long scarves, tap shoes, soft slippers, or socks for dancing. Music is chosen for rhythm and beat and should include slow and fast dances, jiggedy and bouncy dances, and languorous dances.

3. *Playing along.* Simple rhythm instruments are added to the basics of recorded music, and children may "thrum" along with tambourines, sticks, drums, triangles, and cymbals. Suggestions for making certain rhythms may be included; for example, children may be asked to create some rhythms that sound like walking, running, hopping, skipping, or marching.
4. *Creating original music.* Simple, basic instruments are included here so that children may invent their own songs, their own rhythms, their own melody lines.
5. *Making instruments that are pitched.* With eight to twelve glasses or glass jars, a pitcher of water, and metal spoons, children can experiment with sound and pitch, noting how pitch is elevated and lowered. Changing the jars (e.g., different thickness of glass) is likely to generate variations in sounds.
6. *Making instruments that are stringed.* Rubber bands, string, scissors, fine wire, a few cans, several sturdy cardboard containers, wooden strips (about 0.25 by 1.25 inches), and a stapler are primary ingredients for making stringed instruments. Experiments with homemade stringed instruments will yield insights into how pitch is changed as well as into other musical concepts such as vibration, plucking, and bowing.
7. *Playing around with instruments.* While parents and teachers are not likely to place rare and treasured musical instruments into the hands of children, there are instruments that can and should be made available with a few rules and guidelines set down in advance to provide for their care and well-being. In this center children may "fiddle around" with guitars, ukuleles, violins with bows, bongo drums, flutes, recorders, and any other viable wind, percussion or stringed instrument. Learning notation to read music may be accessed on the Internet.

CULINARY ARTS

Some readers may take issue with the inclusion of cooking and baking in the category of "the arts." Julia Child, Alice Waters, and Emeril Lagasse may differ—for to them and others who have risen to culinary fame, creating exceptional cuisine is an art. So without further apologies, this section offers a few suggestions for how young children can create interesting and tasty foods, either at home or at school.

Moreover, using fresh ingredients to create something delicious gives children an appreciation of how foods are prepared and how raw ingredients can be turned into a healthful lunch or snack. The suggestions below range from the easiest to the more complex.

Foods That Can Be Made without an Oven

1. *Butter.* Making butter is perhaps the easiest creative task. It just takes a liter of whipping cream, a large bowl, and either a hand mixer or a beater. Keeping the whipping cream cold helps.
2. *Fruit salad.* Several kinds of fresh fruit, especially what's available in season, can be cut up and mixed in a bowl, topped with yogurt.
3. *Vegetable salad.* Several kinds of fresh vegetables—those that can be eaten raw—can be cut up and mixed in a large bowl: tomatoes, cucumbers, carrots, celery, green pepper, different kinds of lettuce, green beans, radishes, bean sprouts. Bottled dressing may be used, or not. Of course, the children should be able to choose which vegetables to include and how to arrange the ingredients to their best advantage.
4. *Poor person's pizza.* This is easily assembled without needing an oven or even a stove top. Ingredients: English muffins, split, a jar of very good pizza sauce, cheese slices. The children can use the muffins as a pizza base and top them with both the sauces and the cheeses.
5. *Pancakes.* This requires an electric frying pan for easiest use. Ingredients are flour, eggs, milk, baking powder, a little sugar, melted butter, and perhaps blueberries. A nonstick pan will obviate the need for oil to fry the pancakes.

Foods Requiring More Equipment and Preparation

1. *Bread.* Moving into more complex, creative cooking activities, making bread is at the top of the list. A bread-making machine can do the job in a classroom. Ovens are available in some schools in the staff room. Kneading by hand and forming the shapes of the breads gives children a hands-on experience with one of the basic foods of life.
2. *Pizza.* Every child's favorite food, this obviously requires a very hot oven, available in some school staff rooms. But the experience of putting the pizza together before it goes into the oven can be done in a classroom. There are many variations for pizza toppings, and this can be decided by the children prior to shopping for the ingredients.
3. *Apple crisp.* Once again, an oven is required, but the putting together of the ingredients can be done in the classroom: apples, peeled, cored, and sliced; butter, cinnamon, and oatmeal for the topping.
4. *Cookies.* Oven required—but the range of possibilities for cookies is extensive.

AT HOME

Maya and the Cookie Stand: A Story about Creative Cookery at Home

With appreciation to Lin and Maya Snow. (*Note:* Since Maya is nonbinary, her mother uses the nonbinary pronoun in her description.)

A few weeks ago, we attended the evening market in Qualicum Beach. Unlike all of the other local markets, this one is much more free-form. Anyone can set up a table and sell, without needing to sign up, plan in advance, or even pay for a spot! Robert gave each of the kids a five-dollar bill to spend however they wished. But of course, they both ended up at the cotton candy stand, eager to hand their money over for the swirling pink fluff. The vendor had a lineup of kids, and I really admired her clever idea! Besides, there was a lack of treats at the market.

The next week Maya and I talked about putting up a table to sell cookies. They immediately loved the idea and insisted we do it right away! I realized it would give me a chance to take a big step back and let Maya's enthusiasm lead the way. I suggested they write down a cookie sales plan and we could go over it together. They began the plan immediately and sometime later had the list in the figure.

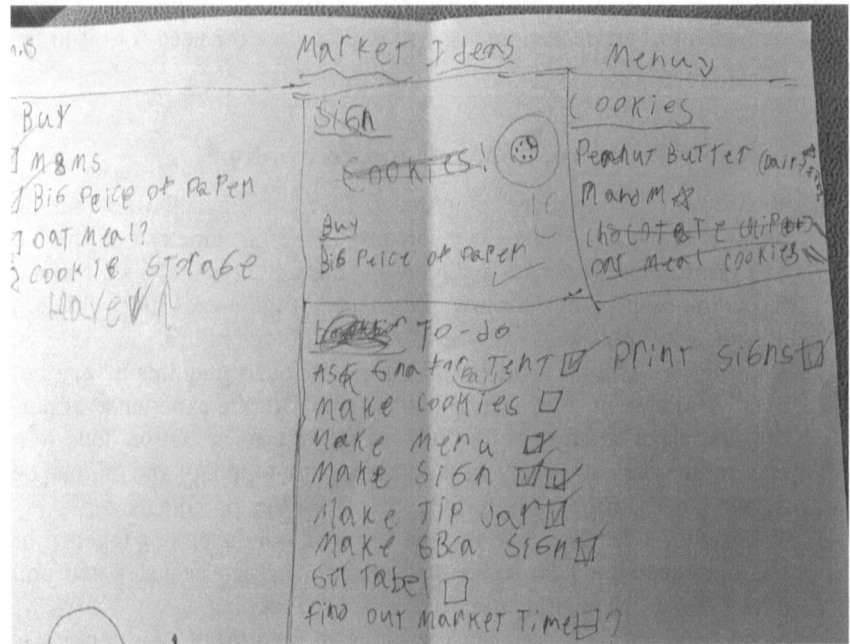

Fig. 7.2. Maya's list. Permission granted by Lin Snow

We reviewed the plan. I suggested that we only bake two types of cookies because four types would take a long time. We decided to make a bigger batch of each peanut butter and M&M (rainbow candy-coated candy). You can see that we worked through Maya's checklist over the next week! This plan was central to our work, and I encouraged them to refer to it often. We had a few cases of "escalating complexity" where their ideas ran away with them. I always agreed to these new plans (bringing a giant bunny to attract attention, using a precious bowl as a tip cup, finding a canopy, etc.). By the day of, Maya had already decided to jettison some of these extra plans and focused on their main goals!

Since we couldn't make cookies immediately, I suggested Maya start with the signs. They used the computer to make two signs. Maya then had to print the signs and use my mom's laminator to protect them. They also used a big piece of paper to make an image of a cookie so that people who couldn't read would understand the signage. Maya chose the BCSPCA (local animal shelter) as the recipient of half of their profits!

For teachers and parents looking for additional recipe suggestions for young children, *Fanny at Chez Panisse* by Alice Walters (1997) is highly recommended.

CONCLUSION

Once again, opportunities for creative, inventive play with the arts are extensive. While what is suggested in this chapter barely scratches the surface of what is possible, the activities at least point in the direction of how creative opportunities can enrich serious play experiences, extending learning horizons for children in unlimited ways.

Chapter 8

Serious Players
Language Arts

Generating ideas for creative play in the language arts should be easy—since virtually all activities have, at the least, an element of speaking, writing, listening, or reading. So choosing from the many alternatives possible presents an embarrassment of riches. Given these options, the activities in this chapter have been shaped within the parameters of acting out, speaking up, becoming literate, reading, writing out, writing down, writing up, and playing games of language and logic. To do all these things better is, of course, a primary language arts goal, not only for the early childhood years but for all children at all ages.

1. PLAYING WITH WORDS AND SOUNDS

Big ideas: Words have auditory and visual relationships to each other. Auditory and visual structures of words give us clues to decoding them.

The learning goals for this activity include experiences with the analysis and manipulation of words; the promotion of awareness of auditory relationships; the promotion of the use of auditory and visual analysis in decoding words.

This activity asks children to use the higher-order thinking skills of observing, comparing, classifying, and interpreting data; examining assumptions; evaluating and judging; making decisions; imagining and inventing.

Materials needed: Words of the following types, written on individual cards. For example: may, say, play, tray, hay, today, hooray, stay; boat, coat, oat, goat, coal, load, oak; loaf, roast, toast; rode, code, bone, hope, hole, home, hose, pole.

Activity Card

Work with a friend and make some observations of the words on the cards. Then think of a good way to classify them.
   What kinds of groups can you make?
   How would each word fit into that group?
   In what other ways might you classify these words?

Debriefing Questions to Follow the Play Activity

Asking children to reflect on their observations:

- What observations did you make about these words?
- How were some of the words alike? How were they different?
- What kinds of groups did you make? How did the words belong to those groups?
- In what other ways could the words be grouped?

Challenging children to think beyond their observations:

- How are the words *road* and *rode* alike? How are they different?
- How do you explain those differences?
- What other words might you add to this group: *hay, say, pay*?
- How are the words *boat* and *coal* alike? How are they different?
- What other words would you add to a group with the words *boat, coal,* and *load*?
- What makes you think those words belong in that group?

Suggestions for Replay

Children may, of course, replay with the same word cards and the original activity card, since many play opportunities are possible with these words. New words of similar types may be added to each group, or new words with different phonetic makeup (*ai* words, *ee* words, *ate* words, *at* words, *it* words, *in* words) may be introduced.

New activity cards may be added for use with any group of words. For example:

- Make some observations of these words. Find some ways to classify them according to the way they sound.
- Make some observations of these words. Find some ways to classify them according to what they mean.

- Make some observations of these words. Find some ways to classify them according to how the vowels sound.
- Make some observations of these words. Try to use them to make up some poems.

Suggestions for More Creative Play

1. Choosing words and acting them out in a pantomime to see if other children can guess the word.
2. Inventing words that rhyme with hard-to-rhyme words like *octopus*, *hippopotamus*, *dinosaur*, *spaghetti*.
3. Playing word games. For example, seeing how many words can be made using these letters:
   C   F   S   R   D   A   O   L   N   H   E
4. Writing as many words as the children can think of that begin or end with the letters *st*.
5. Playing word games such as doing anagrams, unscrambling words, or Scrabble.
6. Writing words in patterns to form the shape of the objects they describe (dogs, cats, houses, violins, balloons).
7. Using blocks or Keva blocks to create words.

2. PLAYING WITH WORD MEANINGS

Big ideas: Words convey meanings. We use words to communicate thoughts and feelings. Some words and phrases convey powerful mental images.

The learning goals for this activity include providing experiences with the analysis of phrases in communicating meaning; promoting awareness of the mental pictures that some words and phrases generate.

This activity asks children to apply the thinking skills of observing, comparing, classifying, and interpreting data; applying principles to new situations; examining assumptions; evaluating and judging; creating and inventing.

Materials needed: Word cards with the following or similar types of phrases: running water, angry lion, singing bird, baby duckling, sad dog, sunset sky, birthday cake, leaping cat, melting snow, silly goose, haunted house, messy room, speeding train, flying saucer, sticky lollipop, wooden bridge, fire truck, ocean waves, roaring elephant, falling down, tough problem, dripping icicles, chocolate ice cream cone, garbage dump, swarm of mosquitoes, hard-boiled egg.

Chapter 8

Fig. 8.1. Kai writes with Lego. Permission granted by Lin Snow

Activity Card

Work with a friend or with a group and make some observations of the phrases on the cards. Then decide on a good way to put them in groups (classify them).

What kinds of groups can you make?
How would each phrase fit into that group?
In what other ways could these phrases be grouped (classified)?

Debriefing Questions to Follow the Play Activity

Asking children to reflect on their observations:

- What observations did you make about these phrases?
- In what ways are the phrases *birthday cake* and *angry lion* alike? How are they different?
- In what ways are the phrases *messy room* and *haunted house* alike? How are they different?
- Can you group these words according to the kinds of pictures they make in your mind? How would you do that?

Challenging children to think beyond their observations:

- What kinds of pictures do you make in your mind when you hear the phrase *running water*? *Melting snow*? *Dripping icicles*?
- When someone tells you that she saw a *flying saucer*, what pictures do you make in your mind? How would you describe the picture you see?
- In what ways are the words *elephant* and *roaring elephant* (*room* and *messy room*; *cake* and *birthday cake*) alike? How are they different?
- What phrases would you add to this group: garbage dump, ugly monster, messy room, yucky food? How do your phrases belong to that group?

Suggestions for Replay

Children may, of course, play again with the phrases in the original activity. New phrases may also be added, or the lot may be replaced with an entirely new set of phrases. Ideally these phrases should come from the children's own language usage, especially expressions used in their daily communications with each other.

New activity cards may be added that reflect other dimensions of words and meanings. For example:

1. Some words make sounds: *choo-choo, ding-ding, hissssss, ding-a-ling, boom-boom*.

    Work with a friend and make up some words that sound like running water, thunder, singing birds, an old car, an angry lion. Write down the words you made.

2. Work with a friend and make up some words and phrases that tell about
   - stars
   - birthdays
   - Saturdays

   Make some notes of your words and phrases.
3. Work with a friend and think of as many words and phrases as you can to describe
   - your morning at school
   - Saturday afternoons

   Make some notes of your words and phrases.
4. Work with a friend and think of as many ways as you can to complete each of these phrases:
   As happy as . . .
   As quiet as . . .
   As ugly as . . .
   As sad as . . .
   As beautiful as . . .
   As alarming as . . .
   As noisy as . . .
   As straight as . . .
   As perfect as . . .
   As embarrassing as . . .
   As round as . . .
   As soft as . . .
   Write the phrases you made.

Suggestions for More Creative Play

1. Acting out: Each child or pair of children chooses a phrase and acts it out in pantomime, while the others try to imagine what the phrase could be.
2. Thinking about words: Children work in pairs and make a list of all the beautiful words they can think of, all the ugly words, all the scary words, all the mean and rotten words, all the kind words.
3. Illustrating words: Many messages are now conveyed by illustrations rather than with words. Children may work in pairs and think of ways to illustrate the following:
   Danger! Thin ice!
   Don't feed the monkeys!
   It's bedtime.
   Clean up your room!
   Stay in the bike lanes.
   Don't forget to feed the dog.

4. Making up and playing out dramas on suggested themes:
   My aunt gave me a new dress for my birthday and I hate it!
   Billy fell off his bicycle and broke his arm.
   The electricity went out right in the middle of my game.
5. Writing e-mail messages: Compose e-mail messages on selected topics.

3. PLAYING WITH WORD POWER

Big ideas: Words are used to convey thoughts and feelings. Some words we hear make us feel good and some make us feel quite bad.

The learning goals for this activity include promoting awareness of the power of language to hurt or help, and to promote appreciation for the ways oral expression is structured to communicate ideas and feelings.

This activity asks children to apply the thinking skills of observing, comparing, and interpreting data; suggesting hypotheses; imagining and inventing; evaluating and judging; making decisions.

Materials needed: Sets of cards with the following types of statements (it is important to avoid using names of children in the class):

I don't want to play with you, Harold.
Look at William. He looks stupid.
Get off that swing, Bernice. It's not your turn.
You can't come to my house.
Fiona is so dumb she thinks that there are really flying saucers.
I don't want Bertha for a partner.
We don't want Marvin in our group.
He can't play on our team.
You can't do anything right.
You'll never get to second grade.
Your picture is stupid. I hate it.
Look at your work. It's a mess.

Activity Card

Make some observations about the statements on all of the cards. Read them to each other and talk together about how they make you feel.

How would you feel if you were William? Harold? Bernice?

How would you feel if you were some of the other children named in these statements?

Why do you suppose people say these mean things?

What ideas do you have to explain it? Talk together and discuss your ideas.

Talk about a time when someone said something mean to you that hurt your feelings.

Put the cards in order, with the meanest one at the top and the least mean one at the bottom.

Debriefing Questions to Follow the Play Activity

Asking children to reflect on their observations:

- What observations did you make about these statements?
- How come words like these can be so hurtful? How do you explain it?
- Will any of you tell about a time when someone said something mean to hurt your feelings? What happens when this occurs?
- In your opinion, which was the meanest statement? Tell why you think that was so mean.

Challenging children to think beyond their observations:

- Why do you suppose people say mean things to each other? What explanations do you have for it?
- When do you say mean things? What happens afterward?
- What's the difference between a mean statement and a nice one? What examples can you give of those differences?

Suggestions for Replay

Sets of new cards with caring, helpful statements may be added. For example:

Oh, William, I hope you can join our team.
I'm so happy to see you.
Harold looks so great with his new haircut.
We want Sarah in our group.
Your poem is so beautiful. I loved it.
I can help you with that. Don't worry.
I'm so happy that you are my friend.
Neil is a good friend to me.
I appreciate you, Lara. You're so cool.
Cole has great ideas.
Abbey is so smart. She helps me with my math when I'm stuck.
I missed you very much when you were absent.

The above statements may be used with the following new activity card:

Make some observations about these statements. Read them out loud to each other and talk about how they make you feel.
How would you feel if you were Abbey? Cole? Lara? Sarah?
Write down some of your ideas about how statements like these make you feel.

Another activity card can be introduced in subsequent replay activities:

Compare the statements:
I can help you with that. Don't worry. / How come you can't do that? It's so easy.
You can't play with us. / I'm so glad you're on our team.
What a stupid shirt. It looks like your pajamas. / What a cool jacket. I wish I had one too.

Suggestions for More Creative Play

1. Drawing pictures that are evoked by words with power to hurt or help.
2. Engaging in dramatic play around themes in which children's statements toward each other are helpful or hurtful.
3. Participating in Appreciation Day or No-Evil-Word Day, in which everyone remembers to say only genuinely nice and kind things to each other.
4. Writing stories or poems on themes related to words with power to hurt or help.

4. PLAYING WITH SPEAKING UP

Big ideas: We talk to each other to communicate our ideas and feelings. Telling each other what we think and how we feel is more "mature" than acting out. Reading and writing are derived from oral language.

The learning goals emphasized in this activity include increasing children's language power; fostering and promoting speech as a medium of expression; helping children to feel more confident in expressing their ideas.

This activity asks children to apply the thinking skills of making decisions; evaluating and judging; summarizing; suggesting hypotheses; examining assumptions.

Materials needed: Pencil and paper for recording ideas; activity cards, each containing just one topic for group discussion. For example:

- Should whales be captured an put into an aquarium?

- What are some good ways to train a dog?
- Are dogs better pets than cats or rabbits?
- What are some of your favorite things?
- My brother (sister) is a pain.
- Should little kids have to do chores?
- How do you suppose birds build their nests?
- What are your favorite foods?
- How do you figure out what to do if you are locked out of your house and your mom won't be home for another hour?
- What's the best way to take care of a pet snake?

The above are just a few suggestions; teachers should feel free to substitute any topics that are more relevant to students' interests. The topics should provide for some emotional involvement for them to be more effective.

Activity Card

Work together and talk about (topic).
 What are your ideas? Write down some of your important ideas.

Debriefing Questions to Follow the Play Activity

Asking children to reflect on their ideas:

- Tell us about some of the ideas you had.
- Tell us why you think that is true.
- Tell us why you believe that is good.
- Tell us more about where you got those ideas.

Challenging children to think beyond their observations:

- Could you give us some examples of what you mean?
- Tell us why you think that would work.
- What do you think might happen if you did that?

Suggestions for Replay

Additional topics may be included for further discussions. Ideas for these new topics can reflect current classroom concerns; the children may be invited to come up with their own topics. Using a recording device to play back some of the discussions can lead to increased insight and awareness not only of the nature of the discussions but also of the ways ideas are being communicated.

Suggestions for More Creative Play

1. Writing stories or poems that arise from group discussions.
2. Creating a class book of poems and stories.
3. Illustrating stories and poems.

5. PLAYING WITH READING AND TELLING STORIES

Big ideas: Stories are descriptions, explanations, reports, tales that are written down. People write stories to give information, to entertain and amuse, to make us think, and to give us pleasure.

The learning goals that are incorporated in this activity include extending children's experiences with story; beginning a process of reading for meaning; increasing appreciation for and pleasure in narratives; developing skill in asking thoughtful, intelligent questions.

This activity asks children to apply the thinking skills of summarizing; interpreting; applying principles to new situations; creating and inventing; evaluating and judging; classifying; suggesting hypotheses.

Materials needed: In this activity the children are asked to bring their own favorite books. Replay requires a recording device and audio stories.

Activity Card

Take turns sharing the story each has brought to the group.
  Tell why you think this is a good story.
  Tell what you liked about it.
  Read aloud one page that is your favorite part.
  When you have finished telling about your story, invite the others in the group to ask you questions about the story.

Debriefing Questions to Follow the Play Activity

Asking children to reflect on their observations:

- Tell about the story you shared.
- Tell about the kind of story it is.
- Tell why you liked it.

Challenging children to think beyond their observations:

- What kind of character was _____? How do you know that it true?

- Why do you suppose _____ did that? How do you explain it?
- What do you see as the "main idea" of this story? What message is the author giving you?
- Why do you think this story is good? What ingredients in the story make it good?

Suggestions for Replay

Replay for this activity occurs naturally as the children continue to bring new books to share.

The children may listen together to a commercially recorded story, accompanied by the book for them to read along. They can discuss the story using questions similar to those on the original activity card.

Other replay activities may include

- Making up and telling original stories.
- Telling stories of things that happened in a child's life.
- Recording original stories.
- Listening to stories with music.

Suggestions for More Creative Play

1. Writing original stories. Since this is one of the major goals of language learning, such activities should be encouraged as much as possible.
2. Illustrating original stories and binding them as books for the classroom library.
3. Creating stories with music.

6. PLAYING WITH WRITING OUT

Big ideas: We write to express our creative imagination, to make visible what we are thinking, feeling, and imagining. Writing is a process of recording oral language.

The learning goals incorporated in this activity are the generation of interest in and appreciation for the telling and writing of original stories and the stimulation of creative imagination and invention as an outlet for thoughts and feelings.

This activity asks children to apply the thinking skills of observing; creating and inventing; evaluating and judging; making decisions; interpreting; summarizing.

Materials needed: Four or five photographs with the potential for evoking deep and powerful affect; an audio recording device; pencil and paper. It's best to use photographs that have some redeeming artistic quality.

Activity Card

Study the photos. Choose one photo that you like.

Talk to each other about the photo.
Then, working together, make up a story about that photo.
When you are all agreed on the story, record it or write it down.

Debriefing Questions to Follow the Play Activity

Asking children to reflect on their observations:

- What did you find in the photo that made you choose it?
- What story did you imagine about the photo?
- What details did you observe in the photo that you liked?

Challenging children to think beyond their observations:

- What kind of story did you create for the photo?
- What do you see as the important message of your story? How is the message in your story similar to the message in the photo?
- What kinds of words might describe this photo?

Suggestions for Replay

New photos may be added to the collection. Photos from family albums, with permission, may also be included. Children may be asked to write captions for the photos. Cartoons may also be added.

Children may share their recorded stories with each other.

Suggestions for More Creative Play

1. Collecting children's original stories into class books.
2. Book illustrating.
3. Book binding.
4. Taking photographs in and around the school that lead to the generation of new stories.

7. PLAYING WITH WRITING DOWN

Big ideas: We use "writing down" to record events, incidents, outcomes, activities—something that happened. We also record information to help people know what to do. We keep records so that information will not be lost, so that we may have it to refer to when we need it. Recording competently is dependent on the accuracy of our observations.

The learning goals incorporated in this activity include developing skill in recording information accurately; promoting appreciation for recorded information as a means of ensuring future reference; raising awareness that events recorded are filtered through our perceptual biases.

This activity asks children to apply the thinking skills of observing and recording; interpreting; evaluating and judging; summarizing.

Materials needed: Pencils and paper.

Activity Card

Go with your group or partner to the school office. On the way there, be careful to observe what route you take and everything you see on the way.

Talk together first and decide what you need to write down about the directions from classroom to office. Then write your observations.

Make sure what you write is clear so that someone else can read it and understand how to follow your directions.

When you have finished writing, take your directions with you and follow what you wrote as you go to the office again.

Check your directions for accuracy. Make any corrections that are needed.

Come back to the classroom and rewrite your directions as necessary.

Debriefing Questions to Follow the Play Activity

Asking children to reflect on their observations:

- What observations did you make about the route from the classroom to the office?
- What observations did you make about anything that was unusual along the way?
- How were these included in your written directions?

Challenging children to think beyond their observations:

- When you followed your directions on the second trip, what did you notice you left out?
- What errors did you make in writing down the directions? How do you explain them?
- How would a person new to your school be able to follow your directions? How would you check that out?
- What's hard about writing directions?

Suggestions for Replay

Children may be asked to write down directions for other routes within the school or outside of the school.

Events may also be recorded, such as those that occur in and around the school, the lunchroom, the library; particular events in the class; a puppet show; the behavior of a pet; an untoward event, like a lost lunch, missing books. Children may be asked to write down events of a personal nature (my grandmother came to visit; we went camping; I lost my tooth; I had a birthday party; my brother punched me in the nose for no reason).

Each group may be asked to record the same event, and the groups can compare different perspectives on the event with this new activity card:

Read each group's description of the event.
How are they different?
What explains the differences?
How do you know which is more accurate?

Replays of writing down can go on throughout the school year. All types of events can and should be recorded, as children gain skill in their ability to observe and record thoughtfully, creatively, and responsibly.

Suggestions for More Creative Play

Starting a class newspaper: The local paper is a good example of what a newspaper contains, as well as what events are recorded and how. Access to word processors may lead to more elegant products, but neatly hand-printed newspapers are also fun, as well as being highly productive thinking and learning experiences.

8. PLAYING WITH CONVERSATION

Big ideas: The way we talk to each other is the essence of human experience. The way we use language can be for better or for worse. Good conversations depend on good listening skills.

The learning goals included in this activity include promoting better understanding of the ways we talk to each other; promoting understanding that words have power to help or to hurt; promoting understanding of the importance of being a good listener; promoting understanding that language is our primary means of human connectivity.

This activity asks children to use the higher-order thinking skills of observing, comparing, and interpreting data; suggesting hypotheses; examining assumptions; creating and inventing.

Materials needed: A collection of five-by-eight-inch index cards containing various conversation "starters" with some emotional weight. Some examples are

- The hurricane is heading our way and I'm worried.
- My big brother always bosses me around.
- I lost my lunch money and I'm afraid to tell my mother.
- I don't like Shirley. She thinks she's smarter than everyone.
- I'm afraid to tell my father that I got a bad mark on my paper.
- My mother only gives me ten minutes for tablet time in the evening.
- I hate having to do chores at home.
- I didn't get picked for the team.
- I'm afraid to tell the teacher that I don't understand the math work.

Activity Card

The cards have some suggestions for topics to talk about. Work with a partner. Pick a topic or invent one of your own, and begin to talk to each other about the topic.

One of you is the "talker."

The other person is the "listener."

The "talker" tells his or her ideas. The "listener" pays careful attention to what the "talker" is saying and tries to say the idea back in a new way, to show that she or he has listened and understands what the "talker" has been saying.

When you have finished talking and listening to each other, talk together and make some observations about your conversation.

What did you observe about how the "listener" helped the "talker."

What did the "listener" do that didn't help the "talker"?
What other observations did you make about the conversation?

Sample Debriefing Questions to Follow the Play

Asking children to reflect on their observations:

- What observations did you make about how the listener helped the talker to talk more about his or her feelings about the topic?
- What observations did you make about how the listener kept missing the meaning of what the "talker" was saying?
- What were some important observations you made about the best ways to talk to each other?

Challenging children to think beyond their observations:

- What do you suppose is hard about listening to someone who is talking to you? What are your ideas about it?
- What do you need to do or say to show a "talker" that you are listening to what she or he is saying?
- Why do you suppose listening to someone is important? What keeps a person from being a good listener? What are your ideas about it?
- What words do people use to hurt someone's feelings? What examples can you give?
- What words do people use to make someone else feel better? What examples can you give?
- How are words used to hurt and help others? What are your ideas about that?

Suggestions for Replay

Children should be encouraged to create new conversations with different topics, changing roles of "talker" and "listener" with each new conversation.

New topics can be added to the collection of cards—reflecting classroom and home issues. These can, of course, be initiated from children's ideas.

Conversations can and should be practiced many times for children to acquire adequate listening and conversation skills.

Suggestions for More Creative Play

1. Creating mini dramas to show good listening skills.

2. Creating mini dramas or puppet shows to show how words are used cruelly.
3. Creating comic strips to show how conversations are helpful or hurtful, to show how poor listening can lead to misunderstandings.
4. Writing poems about the way people talk to each other.

CONCLUSION

The eight language arts activities included in this chapter may be put into direct classroom use. With slight modifications, they may also be used at home. They may also serve as prototypes for what teachers and parents create to satisfy the instructional needs in school or at-home learning situations. In any case, shaping language arts activities in a play-debrief-replay structure contributes to both pleasure and skill development in the language learning of children as well as the building of their skills as self-directed learners.

Chapter 9

Serious Players
Social Studies

The activities included in this chapter are rooted in the broader topics "The Clothes We Wear" and "Jobs and Work." While other social studies topics might have been chosen as well, these two seemed generic in terms of applicability and appropriateness to address some important social studies concerns.

Many of the activities ask for illustrations or photographs to carry out the investigations. Some of these may be acquired from old magazines and newspapers. But an extensive source, easily accessed, is the Internet. These can be printed out and mounted, making the task of finding suitable materials much easier.

1. PLAYING WITH THE CLOTHES WE WEAR

Big ideas: Most of the clothes we wear are manufactured. Our clothes have different functions.

The learning goals for this activity include promoting awareness of how clothes are made and how different clothes are appropriate for different situations.

This activity asks children to use the higher-order thinking skills of observing, comparing, and classifying data; suggesting hypotheses; imagining and inventing; evaluating and judging; designing investigations; making decisions.

Materials needed: A selected sampling of children's and adults' articles of clothing: tie, belt, suspenders, jacket, gloves, hat, sweater, jeans, T-shirt, socks, coat, rainwear, heavy coat, bathing suit, shorts; pictures of clothes. More "exotic" clothes: robes, headdresses, clothes from yesteryear, togas, costumes. Hats may be included if available. Children may also make contributions to this collection. Clothes may be scrounged from sources such as thrift stores and secondhand stores. Only a selected few need to be included in one play activity.

Activity Card

Use the materials in the center to find out what you can about these clothes.

Make some observations about how these clothes are made. What kinds of fabrics are used? How are the clothes put together? What kinds of differences can be observed in them?

Make some observations about the purposes for which some of these clothes are worn. Then talk together and think of a good way to classify these articles of clothing. Which belong together? Which can be left out? How do you explain your choices?

Debriefing Questions to Follow the Play Activity

Asking children to reflect on their observations:

- What observations did you make about these articles of clothing?
- What observations did you make about how they are made? About what they are made of? About what they are worn for? About shapes and sizes?

Challenging children to think beyond their observations:

- Which articles of clothing did you like better? Less? How do you explain the difference?
- Where do you suppose these clothes are made? How do you know? How can you tell?
- Which would you like better: a shirt of cotton or a shirt of polyester? What's the difference? How do you know that is true?
- Why do some men wear ties? What are they good for? How do you know?
- Why do you suppose we dress up for special occasions? What does "dressing up" mean?
- Why do you suppose "old fashioned" clothes look silly to us now? What are your ideas about that?
- What's the purpose of wearing a hat? How do you know that is true?
- Where do the fabrics come from? How are they colored? How do they get those designs? What are your ideas?

- How come some people want to wear clothes with designer labels that cost more than the same clothes without the labels? How do you explain this?

Suggestions for Replay

The children may replay with the same articles of clothing and the original activity card. New articles of clothing may be added (knitted garments, woven garments, scarves or shawls, fur pieces, a muff, gym clothes), as can photos of clothing from earlier years.

New activity cards may be added. For example:

1. Go around the classroom and observe the label in everyone's shirt, or sweater, or jeans. Make a list of the countries in which these articles of clothing have been made. Then design a chart to show this information.
2. Work together and figure out a new way to make a pattern for a T-shirt. Make the pattern.
3. Work together and make some observations of the different kinds of fabric used in the manufacture of clothing. Make a list of all the fabrics. Then classify the list by putting them into groups.
4. Design an article of clothing that might be used by a visitor from outer space. Talk together and make some drawing of your design. Decide what kinds of fabrics, colors, and adornments the clothing will have.

Pictures cut out from the latest fashion magazine may be added, along with the following new activity card:

Make some observations of these pictures of "latest fashion" clothes.
Which did you like? Which did you dislike?
What makes clothes attractive?
How do you suppose new fashion designs for your clothes are created?
　What makes them popular? What are your ideas about that?

Suggestions for More Creative Play

1. Growing a cotton plant.
2. Dying fabric with natural dyes; making batik.
3. Textile printing.
4. Weaving, knitting, or sewing.
5. Engaging in dramatic play with costumes.
6. Designing costumes.

7. Imagining and creating what clothes will look like one hundred years from now.

2. PLAYING WITH THE SHOES WE WEAR

Big ideas: Shoes come in various styles, sizes, and shapes. Different shoes have different functions.

The learning goals for his activity include promoting awareness of different styles, materials used, and functions of certain kinds of shoes.

This activity asks children to use the higher-order thinking skills of observing and comparing; suggesting hypotheses; classifying; imagining and inventing; evaluating and judging.

Materials needed: A collection of shoes: rain boots, sneakers, running shoes, sandals, sports shoes, work boots, shoes with laces, shoes with high heels, snowshoes, slippers, moccasins, booties, snow boots, platform shoes; photos or pictures of shoes worn in earlier centuries. Children may also be asked to bring in old or discarded shoes from home, thrift stores, and yard sales.

Activity Card

Use the materials in this center to make some observations of shoes.

How are the shoes different from each other? How are they alike? What similarities and differences can you discover?

Talk together and think of a good way to classify these shoes. Which ones belong together? How come?

Sample Debriefing Questions to Follow the Play Activity

Asking children to reflect on their observations:

- What observations did you make about these shoes? About their styles? About the material used to make them? About how they are made? About what we wear them for?
- What differences did you observe about them? What similarities?

Challenging children to think beyond their observations:

- Which shoes do you suppose are "old fashioned"? How can you tell?
- What do you suppose "old fashioned" means?

- How come shoe styles change over the years? What are your ideas about that?
- What's the purpose of some of these shoes? How can you tell that is true?
- What do you think shoes will look like in one hundred years? Try to imagine it.

Suggestions for Replay

The children may play with the same materials and the original activity card until they lose interest in the tasks.

For later replays with the original activity card, the children may be given new shoes and pictures of shoes (high-style shoes; baby shoes; shoes from other cultures, such as wooden shoes and clogs, mukluks, military boots, booties, ballet slippers, running shoes; horseshoes).

New activity cards that focus on different aspects of shoes may be introduced. For example:

Make some observations of how shoes are made. What kinds of materials are needed? How are the materials put together to make the shoes?

Make some observations of how different shoes feel when you wear them. Which shoes feel good on the feet? Which hurt your feet? Which are easy to walk in? Hard to walk in?

Which look beautiful? Ugly?

Which keep your feet warmer? Cooler?

Which are good to wear for working? Playing soccer? Riding a bike?

How are shapes of shoes and shapes of feet alike?

How are horseshoes different from running shoes? What do you see as some important differences?

Suggestions for More Creative Play

1. Drawing pictures of shoes.
2. Imagining what the first pairs of shoes worn by early people looked like and drawing pictures of them.
3. Designing shoes for space travel.
4. Making shoes out of fabric and heavy-duty cardboard.
5. Dramatizing stories about shoes ("The Shoemaker and the Elves") or creating original plays about shoes.
6. Creating a mural of the imprints of children's feet. (This is a messy activity but a lot of fun.)

3. PLAYING WITH FABRIC

Big ideas: Fabrics are woven cloths. Many different kinds of fabrics, natural and synthetic, are used in the manufacture of clothing.

The learning goals for this activity include promoting understanding of the kinds of fabrics that go into the making of the clothes we wear; to develop awareness of how fabric is made.

This activity asks children to use the higher-order thinking skills of observing, comparing, and classifying; examining assumptions; suggesting hypotheses; evaluating and judging; making decisions.

Materials needed: An assortment of fabrics (velvet, cotton, felt, terry cloth, silk, rayon, polyester, velour, corduroy, brocade, chiffon); fabrics with different textures, thicknesses, and prints; needles, thread, scissors.

Activity Card

Use the materials in this center to find out what you can about these different fabrics.

What observations can you make about them? How are they alike?

What differences can you observe about texture? Softness? Thickness? Print? Weave?

What other differences can you see?

How might these fabrics be classified? What kinds of groups could be set up?

Debriefing Questions to Follow the Play Activity

Asking children to reflect on their observations:

- What observations did you make about these fabrics? About their texture? Thickness? Softness? Weave? Design?
- What similarities did you find? What differences?
- How did you classify the pieces of fabric? How did each piece of fabric belong in that group?

Challenging children to think beyond their observations:

- How do you suppose fabric is made? What are your ideas about this?
- Where do you suppose silk (cotton, leather) comes from? What are your ideas about this?

- Where do you suppose velvet (felt, polyester) comes from? What are your ideas about this?
- How do you suppose they get the designs and colors onto the fabric? What are your ideas about this?
- What fabrics are good for making jackets (trousers, dresses, shirts)? What are your ideas about this? What makes you think your ideas are true?

Suggestions for Replay

Children may replay with the same materials and the original activity card until their interest is exhausted. Then the original card may be used with new fabrics (fur, leather, knitted fabrics).

Raw materials (balls of wool, spools of textile threads, weaving cards) may be added, along with photographs of the spinning of thread and the manufacture of textiles and clothing. The following activities may be introduced in conjunction with these new materials:

- Work together and use the materials in the center to make an article of clothing.
- Make some observations about how cloth is woven. Use the materials in the center to weave some cloth.

Suggestions for More Creative Play

1. Designing patterns for clothing.
2. Sewing, knitting, weaving.
3. Making patchwork quilts.
4. Making cloth hand puppets.
5. Making fabric mobiles and fabric collages.
6. Tie-dyeing fabrics.

4. PLAYING WITH CLOTHING STYLES

Big ideas: Clothes change in style. What was fashionable years ago looks silly to us today. Sometimes people are judged by the clothes they wear.

The learning goals for this activity include promoting awareness of the idea of "style" in clothing as a reflection of cultural standards and values.

This activity asks children to use the higher-order thinking skills of observing and comparing; evaluating and judging; suggesting hypotheses; examining assumptions; imagining and creating; making decisions.

Materials needed: Photographs and illustrations of "fashionable" apparel dating back several centuries. Such photos and illustrations of clothing worn in earlier decades can be obtained from old magazines found in used book shops, in old textbooks, and of course on the Internet. Examples could be cut out and mounted on cardboard so that they may be handled without being torn. Examples of men's, women's, and children's clothing should be included.

Activity Card

Make some observations of the clothes in these pictures.

What observations can you make about the styles of clothing that were worn long ago?

What observations can you make about how the styles of men's (women's, children's) clothing have changed over the years? Talk together about what you have observed.

What do you see as some important differences in the designs of the clothes? Trousers? Shoes? Hats? The lengths of the dresses? Colors? The shapes of the dresses? Jackets?

Debriefing Questions to Follow the Play Activity

Asking children to reflect on their observations:

- What observations did you make about the kinds of clothes that were worn long ago?
- How were these clothes (at a particular time) different from ours?
- What do you see as some important differences about the styles of women's (children's) dresses? Shoes? Hats?

Challenging children to think beyond their observations:

- How come these clothes of long ago look so funny to us today? How do you explain this? What are your ideas?
- What do you suppose our clothes will look like in the future? Can you imagine this? What are your ideas?
- How do clothes get designed? Who makes up the ideas for the design of clothing? How does this work?
- What can you tell about people from looking at what they wear? What are your ideas about this? Is it good, do you think, to make judgments about people based on what they wear?

- What makes clothes "plain"? What makes them "fancy"? What are your ideas about that?
- Why do you suppose some people like to dress up in "fancy" clothes? In costumes? What are your ideas about that?

Suggestions for Replay

Children's interest in the original activity is likely to be sustained over several replay sessions with the same photos and illustrations, using the same activity card. New photos and illustrations may be added for use with the original activity card or with new activity cards. For example:

- How might these photos of clothes be classified? Talk together and decide how they might be grouped. What are some other ways to classify the photos?
- Compare the pictures of clothes worn by children one hundred years ago with the pictures of clothes worn now. How did children's clothing change? What do you see as some important differences?
- Observe the photos of clothes. What can you tell about the people who are wearing them? Talk together and see what you can observe about them.
- What do you suppose different kinds of hats tell you about the people who wear them? What are your ideas about this?

Suggestions for More Creative Play

1. Dressing up in costumes of yesteryear.
2. Engaging in dramatic play in old-fashioned clothes.
3. Dramatizing stories about clothes ("The Emperor's New Clothes," "Cinderella").
4. Imagining and inventing clothes for space travel.
5. Creating the most outrageous Halloween costume.
6. Drawing and illustrating different kinds of hats worn on different occasions.
7. Writing stories and poems on suggested topics (I wanted a new dress for the party; They laughed at my funny clothes; I hated my new shoes).
8. Making and dressing puppets and putting on a puppet show.

5. PLAYING WITH JOBS AND WORK

Big ideas: People work at different kinds of jobs. Different jobs require different talents, skills, and abilities. Certain jobs bring certain satisfactions and dissatisfactions.

The learning goals promoted in this activity include developing awareness of the different kinds of jobs and occupations that provide income; developing appreciation for the variety and complexity of work and job opportunities.

This activity asks children to use the higher-order thinking skills of observing, comparing, classifying, and interpreting data; evaluating and judging; suggesting hypotheses; examining assumptions; imagining and inventing.

Materials needed: A collection of photos of men and women at work at different jobs (dentist, sailor, taxi driver, salesperson, coal miner, construction worker, baker, farmer, auto mechanic, secretary, teacher, pilot, police officer, member of clergy, painter, sculptor, musician, fisher, football player, technician, IT specialist, plumber, astronaut, tailor, physicist, repair person, hotel clerk, baker, doctor, railroad engineer, office worker, film star, firefighter, carpenter, photographer, nurse, bus driver, clown). Ensure that photos are nonsexist in their references to who holds what jobs.

Activity Card

Use the photos in this center to make some observations about the kind of work that people do. Talk to each other about what you think these jobs are like.

What do you think it's like to work as an artist? A baker? A farmer? A pilot? A taxi driver? What are your ideas about this?

What's good about those kinds of jobs? What might you not like about them?

Think of a way to classify these job pictures. Set up some groups and put each picture in the group where you think it belongs.

Debriefing Questions to Follow the Play Activity

Asking children to reflect on their observations:

- What observations did you make about the kinds of work these people are doing?
- What do you suppose it's like to work as a farmer? Baker? Plumber? Construction worker? Railroad engineer?
- What's good about that job? What are some things you might not like?

- Why do you suppose people choose the jobs they do? What are your ideas about this?

Challenging children to think beyond their observations:

- What kinds of groups did you make for the job pictures? What other kinds of groups might have been made?
- How come some people choose dangerous jobs, like working on building bridges or tall buildings, or coal mining? What are your ideas about that?
- What happens when people cannot find jobs? What are some of your ideas about that?
- What kind of job would you like to do when you grow up? Tell why you think you might like that work.
- Why do you suppose people work? What's the importance of work in one's life? What are your ideas about that?
- What do you think you need to do in order to become a pilot (or any other job that requires extensive training)? How is it different from working at a fast-food restaurant? How do you know this is true?
- How come some jobs have lots of men working at them (like pilots, engineers, IT specialists) while others have mostly women (like nurses)? How do you explain this? What are your ideas?
- How do you suppose jobs and work have changed over the last one hundred years? What kinds of jobs did people do then? What are your ideas about this?
- In some countries, children as young as ten years old are required to work at hard jobs, for very little pay. How do you suppose that is possible? What are your ideas about this?

Suggestions for Replay

The children may replay with the same photos setting up other classifications.

New photos or other kinds of illustrations of people at work (veterinarian, forest ranger, migrant worker, lighthouse keeper, oil rig worker, zoo attendant, lion tamer, ship's captain, pharmacist, lab technician, chemist, astronomer) may be added for use with the original activity card or with new activity cards.

Photos showing the jobs that people did a century ago (milk delivery man in a horse and wagon; laundry worker; maid; servant; telephone operator; farmer; doctor; tailor; baker; miner; sweatshop workers; textile worker; factory worker) can be observed and compared to current jobs and working conditions. (The Internet is a good source for photos of these older jobs and the working conditions under which many lower-paid people worked.)

Photos of child labor can be accessed on the Internet. Another option is learning about the life and work of Craig Keilburger, a young Canadian boy who was an anti-child-labor activist.

Questions about these can include

1. Compare the job of a veterinarian to the job of a zookeeper. How are they alike? How are they different? Talk about all the similarities and differences you can think of.
2. Compare the job of a teacher with working as an actor. How are these jobs alike? How are they different? Talk about the similarities and differences you can think of.
3. Compare the work of a doctor (dentist, factory worker) one hundred years ago with their work today. What do you see as some important differences?
4. What do you see as some advantages of using child labor, as they do in certain countries? What do you see as some disadvantages?

The children may participate in a role-playing activity in which each child in the group chooses a part in one of the following types of scenarios: a visit to the dentist's office; working as a cashier in the supermarket; working together to build a house; a flight crew on an airplane going to Alaska; a staff of newspaper workers trying to get the newspaper out on time.

Suggestions for More Creative Play

1. Drawing or painting pictures about people at work at different jobs.
2. Writing stories or poems about working at different jobs.
3. Acting out scenarios such as those in the role-play activity above.
4. Singing and dancing to folksongs with a job or work theme ("I've Been Working on the Railroad," "I Owe My Soul to the Company Store," "Come Mr. Tally Man, Tally Me Banana," "Sweet Molly Malone").

6. PLAYING WITH WORK AND PAY

Big ideas: Some jobs are highly paid. Others are poorly paid. Some jobs carry higher status.

The learning goals for this activity include promoting awareness of the range of income connected to certain jobs; promoting understanding of the relationship between work, income, and status.

This activity asks children to use the higher-order thinking skills of observing, comparing, classifying, and interpreting data; examining assumptions;

evaluating and judging; suggesting hypotheses; imagining and inventing; making decisions.

Materials needed: The same collection of jobs and work photographs used for Activity 5 may be used again for this task, but the photos should be divided into two groups: higher-income jobs and lower-income jobs. Choose about six photos for each group.

Activity Card

The photographs in this center have been grouped into two categories. In Group 1 you see people working at jobs where they earn higher incomes. In Group 2 you see people working at jobs where they earn lower incomes. Study the photos in these two groups.

What observations can you make about higher-paying and lower-paying jobs?

Talk together about what you observe about these jobs.

What can you tell from your observations about why people working at jobs in Group 1 are making much more money than those working at jobs in Group 2?

Debriefing Questions to Follow the Play Activity

Asking children to reflect on their observations:

- What observations did you make about the jobs in Group 1?
- What observations did you make about the jobs in Group 2?
- What are some important differences about these two groups of jobs?

Challenging children to think beyond their observations:

- How come a famous football star earns much more money than a teacher? What are your ideas about this? How do you explain it?
- Is it better to have a job that pays you lots of money? What are your ideas about that?
- Should famous singers earn more money than firefighters? What do you think? What are your ideas about this?
- What kinds of jobs should pay the most money? What are your ideas?
- What might be some advantages of having a high paying job? What might be some disadvantages?

Suggestions for Replay

Two new sets of photos may be used that are grouped, once again, into the same categories, along with the original activity card.

Role-playing activities may be added, with each child in the group choosing a part to play in one of the following scenarios: a movie star comes to visit your classroom; a maid wants a job in a fancy house; the young daughter in a family wants to take a dangerous job; your friend has a boring job as a dishwasher; a friend doesn't earn enough money at her job as a newspaper delivery person; people think a friend's job walking the dogs is silly.

Suggestions for More Creative Play

1. Drawing or painting men, women, and children at work at certain jobs.
2. Writing stories or poems about jobs and work.
3. Engaging in dramatic play and role-play about jobs and work.
4. Pantomiming to express certain job functions (this could be done as charades).

CONCLUSION

The six activities in this section do not represent a total social studies curriculum for primary graders. They do, however, provide for rich investigative experiences with selected social studies issues. As well, they give examples of how other investigative play opportunities may be created.

These activities are also easily applicable to home studies, some requiring only minor modifications. The burden for parents is the effort needed to gather the materials for the investigative plays. As mentioned above, the Internet is a valuable and reliable source for obtaining many of the photographs needed. Soliciting children's help in gathering the materials may have added benefits.

Parents are also encouraged to use these activities as examples to design other issue-related social studies investigations.

Chapter 10

Serious Players

Science

Science is everywhere around us, from the early morning fog that immobilizes the airport to the burned toast; from Facebook and Twitter to the first robin of spring; from your laptop computer to the five pounds you gained on summer vacation. Whether it's popsicles, pearls, butterflies, or popcorn, it's science. Whether it's the weather, toxic waste, or the moon, it's science. What can children do to increase their understanding of science? Everything! The options are virtually unlimited (Wassermann and Ivany 2022).

The activities included in this chapter offer children opportunities to carry on scientific investigations leading to increased concept development. None of them directs children to find the "right" answers, nor do they stress the acquisition of specific information. Instead, children are encouraged to inquire, to exercise their higher-order thinking skills, to compare and observe, to imagine and invent and design experiments, and to decide. Through these investigative experiences, scientific thinking grows, as does scientific awareness and understanding.

These activities are not concerned with teaching children that water boils at a temperature of 212 degrees Fahrenheit; rather, they are concerned with teaching children how to find out the boiling temperature of water—and further, why that temperature might vary in different locations. Learning science is learning to question, not to accept given information as fact or truth.

It is on those principles that the activities included in this chapter are based. The big ideas of the activities chosen for this chapter include:

- Living things grow and change.
- Plants and animals are living things.
- Machines and tools help us do work.
- Our senses are used to discover the properties of objects.
- Technology has become increasingly important in our lives.

Certainly, other activities based on other big ideas could have been chosen; however, these seemed to be suitable and appropriate to learning in the primary years.

1. PLAYING WITH SEEDS AND PLANTS

Big ideas: Living things grow and change.

The learning goals for this activity include promoting understanding of the ways plants grow and change; increasing skill in learning to make thoughtful observations from data; learning to classify data.

This activity asks children to use the higher-order thinking skills of observing, comparing, and classifying data; suggesting hypotheses; creating and inventing; making decisions; applying principles to new situations; designing investigations.

Materials needed: A variety of seeds (flower, fruit, and vegetable seeds; birdseed; seeds from trees such as fir cones, acorns, chestnuts); an assortment of fresh flowers and leaves; an assortment of dried flowers and leaves; photographs of flowers, plants, and trees in bud, in full bloom, and dormant; magnifying lenses, scissors, measuring tools, knives.

Activity Card

Use the materials to find out what you can about how plants grow and change.

What observations can you make about these seeds? Where do you suppose the seeds come from?

What observations have you made about how the seeds make flowers (plants, trees) grow?

What observations can you make about how flowers (plants, trees) change as they grow?

Make some observations and then decide how these seeds, plants, and flowers can be classified.

Debriefing Questions to Follow the Play Activity

Asking children to reflect on their observations:

- What observations did you make about the seeds?
- What observations did you make about how plants grow?
- What observations did you make about how plants change?
- In what ways did you classify these seeds, plants, and flowers? Tell your reasons for making those groups.

Challenging children to think beyond their observations:

- What are some differences you found among flower, fruit, and vegetable seeds? What are some similarities?
- What makes seeds grow? What hypotheses can you suggest to explain this?
- Where do you suppose seeds come from? What are your ideas?
- How come some trees lose all their leaves in the winter and grow again in the spring? How do you explain this? How does it happen?

Suggestions for Replay

The children may replay with the same materials and the original activity card.

New seeds (nuts in shells, like peanuts, sunflower seeds, almonds, pecans, dried beans) may be added along with a new activity card. But *caution*: Some schools expressly sanction peanuts as many children are allergic to them. Be especially wary if some children have allergies to certain nuts.

These prompts can be added with a new activity card:

Use these materials to make some observations about these seeds.
What observations can you make about the nut seeds?
How are they like flower seeds? How are they different?

Fresh fruits and vegetables (cucumbers, apples, peas, cherries, green peppers, string beans, squashes, pumpkins) may be added, along with the following activity card:

Use these materials to make some observations about fruit and vegetable seeds.
What observations did you make about the seeds?
How are they like nut seeds? How are they different?
How do seeds get into the vegetables and fruits? How do you explain it? What are your ideas?

Some longer-term investigations might also be carried out, such as growing plants from seeds, caring for classroom plants, planting and caring for a garden, and adopting a neighborhood tree and looking after its care.

Suggestions for More Creative Play

1. Making crepe-paper flowers, jewelry from seeds, mosaics by painting seeds or beans and gluing them on paper.

2. Drawing and painting flowers, plants, and trees.
3. Cooking with fruits, vegetables, and dried legumes.
4. Making dyes from vegetables, fruits, and legumes.

2. PLAYING WITH LIVING AND NONLIVING THINGS

Big ideas: Plants are living things.

The learning goals for this activity include promoting understanding of the concept "living things"; promoting awareness that living things need certain conditions in which to grow; increasing skill in learning to make thoughtful observations from data; developing skill in suggesting hypotheses based on logical interpretations of data.

This activity asks children to use the higher-order thinking skills of observing, comparing, classifying, and interpreting data; suggesting hypotheses; making decisions; applying principles; imagining; designing projects and investigations.

Materials needed: A variety of "started" vegetable sprouts (lima beans, mung beans, alfalfa, potato, sweet potato, onion, radish, carrot tops); cuttings from several house plants; several inanimate objects (rocks and stones, pieces of plastic, marbles, balls, rubber bands); dissecting knives; magnifying lenses; paper towels; growing dishes.

Activity Card

Use the materials to make some observations about living and nonliving things.

What observations have you made?

What are some important differences you observed between living and nonliving things?

Sample Debriefing Questions to Follow the Play Activity

Asking children to reflect on their observations:

- What observations did you make about what is alive?
- In what ways are these living things alike? What are some common features?
- How are living things different from nonliving things? How did you determine this?

Challenging children to think beyond their observations:

- How do living things grow? What are your ideas about this? What observations did you make that allow you to make those statements?
- In what ways do living things change? What observations did you make about this?
- How can you tell if something is living? What do you look for? What are your ideas?
- In what ways are living plants like living animals? How are they different?
- Where do you suppose nonliving things come from? What are your ideas?

Suggestions for Replay

Replay may occur with the same materials and the original activity card. Additional materials of living and nonliving things (flower seeds, growing plants, leaf cuttings, branches from trees, soil, sand, water, plates, cups, utensils) may be added for use with the original activity card.

The children may be given the opportunity to observe live animals (white mice, gerbils, hamsters, guinea pigs, snakes, rabbits, insects) with either of the following new activity cards:

Make some observations of the mice (gerbils, hamsters).

- What can you observe about what these animals need to stay alive?
- What helps them grow? How do you know this?
- What harms their growth? How do you know this?

Make some observations of the mice (gerbils, hamsters).

- How are living animals like living plants?
- What similarities do you observe? What differences?

The children may be given seeds for planting (grapefruit, orange, lima bean, mung bean, squash, or flower seeds) with the following new activity card:

Plant some seeds and make some observations about how living things grow.

- What do they need to help them grow? What observations have you made about this?
- What harms their growth? What observations have you made about this?

For another type of planting and growing activity, root vegetables (potato, sweet potato, carrot, turnip) may be added for use with an activity card similar to the one above.

Pictures of living things (plants, trees, flowers, fruits, vegetables, different species of animals) may be gathered for children to classify or compare.

For more long-term investigations, children may grow seeds under different experimental conditions: no water versus adequate water; no sunlight versus adequate sunlight versus too much sunlight; poor soil versus good soil; too hot/cold versus proper temperature.

Suggestions for More Creative Play

1. Writing or telling stories with a "life" focus (Once I was a baby but now I am a big boy [girl]; The day my dog had puppies; Growing old means getting a lot of wrinkles).
2. Growing a garden, with children planning together and gathering the necessary materials; in schools or homes in urban centers plans may include planting in large-size window boxes.
3. Participating in arts and crafts projects such as painting and drawing plants, flowers, and animals; making dyes from plants and vegetables (beets, carrots, onions).
4. Cooking and tasting foods made from things that grow from seeds, such as popping corn; roasting pumpkin seeds.
5. Nature walks. This is probably more conducive to schools and homes in more rural areas. If such walks are possible, children may bring along sketch pads, pencils, and felt pens to make drawings that record what they observe.

3. PLAYING WITH LIVE ANIMAL STUDIES

Big ideas: Living things grow and change.

The learning goals in this activity include promoting understanding of the ways living animals grow and change; promoting attitudes of respect for living creatures; increasing skill in learning to make thoughtful observations from data; increasing observational skills.

This activity asks children to use the higher-order thinking skills of observing, comparing, classifying, and interpreting data; making decisions; evaluating and judging; designing projects and investigations.

Materials needed: One or more animals that can easily be housed in the classroom (or home): hamster, white mice, rabbit, snake, lizard, gerbil, guinea pig, bird, tropical fish; an appropriate "home" for the pet, one that provides the most natural environment; adequate food and water; a timer, watch, or clock.

Activity Card

Study the animal for a long time. What observations have you made?
   What have you observed about its shape? Color? Skin or fur? Tail?
   What observations have you made about how it moves? How it hears? How it sees? How it makes sounds? How and what it eats?
   What observations have you made about how the animal behaves when it thinks it's in danger?

Sample Debriefing Questions to Follow the Play

Asking children to reflect on their observations:

- What observations did you make about this animal?
- What observations did you make about what it eats? How it eats? How often it eats?
- What observations did you make about what it drinks? How it drinks? How often it drinks?
- What observations did you make about how it protects itself from danger?
- What observations did you make about how it moves? How it uses its tail? How it breathes? How it sees? How it hears? How it makes sounds?

Challenging children to think beyond their observations:

- In what ways is the animal like other animals in this species? How is it different?
- What ideas do you have about how to keep this animal healthy and safe? What are your thoughts on this? Where do those ideas come from?
- What observations have you made about how this animal grows?
- What hypotheses can you suggest about how this animal cares for its young? Where do your ideas come from?
- How do you suppose this animal communicates with its young? What are your ideas?
- How do you suppose this animal feels about being in your classroom (home)? What are your ideas? Where do those ideas come from?
- Do animals have feelings? What evidence do you have to support your ideas?

Suggestions for Replay

There is much to be gained if the children repeat the live-animal studies using the original activity card.

Another animal of a different species (insect, turtle, chick, earthworm) may be introduced for study and comparison, along with any of the following activity cards:

Study the turtle (spider, earthworm). Make some observations about this animal.

- What do you observe about the way it moves? Gets its food? Eats?
- What do you observe about its shape? Color? Eyes? Ears?
- What do you observe about how it behaves when it thinks it's in danger?
- How is this animal like _____? How is it different?

Study the turtle (snake, rabbit).

- What do you think its life is like?
- How would you describe a day in the life of this animal?

Photos of animals from sources like *National Geographic* and *Wildlife* magazines and the Internet may be gathered for children to classify. In addition, children may compare photos of pairs of animals (chimpanzees and dogs; dinosaurs and snakes; dolphins and octopuses; kangaroos and camels).

Animal bones (chicken, beef, fish) may be added for children to study. These can be obtained from washing and drying out the bones left from meals. Children may also do dissections of, for example, squid, beef hearts, kidneys, or fish. Such materials can be obtained from local butcher shops or fish stores.

Suggestions for More Creative Play

1. Participating in arts and crafts projects, such as making animals from clay or papier-mâché; drawing and painting pictures of animals.
2. Writing original poetry or stories about animals.
3. Writing or telling stories that speculate about the disappearance of dinosaurs; animals in zoos versus animals in the wild; fears of animals.
4. Engaging in dramatic play on suggested animal themes (We are the animals in the zoo; Me and my pet rhinoceros; We are the gorillas living in the jungle; I'm a very shy koala and I live in a eucalyptus tree), as well as inventing original scenarios about animals.

4. PLAYING WITH WHEELS AND GEARS

Big ideas: Machines and tools make our work easier.

The learning goals for this activity include promoting understanding of how machines extend human capabilities to "do work"; appreciating the effectiveness of machines to perform certain functions; increasing awareness that the motion of a machine requires energy; increasing skill in learning to observe critically and analytically; making intelligent comparisons; suggesting reasonable hypotheses that are borne out by data.

This activity asks children to use the higher-order thinking skills of observing and comparing; suggesting hypotheses; designing investigations; evaluating and judging; making decisions.

Materials needed: A supply of wheels and gears of various sizes and constructions (rubber wheels, plastic wheels, metal wheels and axles, bicycle wheels, toy automobile tires, wagon wheels, roller skates, wheels from children's toys); gear assemblies from such household appliances as a manual pencil sharpener, an eggbeater, a windup clock; heavy objects to move (bricks, cinder blocks, large pieces of wood); large plastic or wooden tubs, buckets, pails of sand and water, flat wooden boards.

Activity Card

Use the materials to make some studies of wheels and gears.

What observations can you make about how wheels work? How gears work?

What observations can you make about how wheels are built? How gears are built?

What observations can you make about how wheels are used to move things? How gears are used to move things?

Sample Debriefing Questions to Follow the Play Activity

Asking children to reflect on their observations:

- What observations have you made about wheels? Gears?
- What observations have you made about how wheels are made to turn? How gears are made to turn?
- What observations have you made about how wheels make our work easier? How gears make our work easier?

Challenging children to think beyond their observations:

- How do you suppose wheels and gears help us to move things? How can you explain this?
- What makes a wheel or gear move more easily? What are your ideas?
- What kinds of machines need wheels? Gears? How do these tools help the machines move? What are your ideas?
- How are gears different from wheels? How are they alike?
- What are some differences between ice skates and roller skates? Between bicycles and wagons?
- If we didn't have wheels to help us move these large and heavy cinder blocks, what might we do instead? What ideas do you have about that?

Suggestions for Replay

There are many other investigations that children may still conduct with the same materials and the original activity card. As well, new materials may be added for use with the original activity card (pulley with rope and hook, bicycle, toy trucks and cars).

New materials may be added for making comparisons (eggbeater and a wire whisk; sled and wagon; toy truck and sailboat).

New activity cards may be added that call for investigating ways to move heavy equipment across the classroom; to study differences between wheeled/geared and nonwheeled/nongeared vehicles or tools; to study how wheels and gears are used in toys.

New activity cards may be added that call for making lists of machines and equipment around the school that are wheel- or gear-driven and the setting up of classification systems for the items on the list.

Suggestions for More Creative Play

1. Writing or telling stories about tools and machines on suggested topics (My brother thinks he's a big wheel; My friend got stuck on the Ferris wheel: There are one hundred wheels in a merry-go-round).
2. Designing and building an exercise wheel for a class pet or a wagon to carry blocks.
3. Drawing pictures of things with big wheels or gears (Ferris wheel, merry-go-round).

5. PLAYING WITH SIMPLE TOOLS

Big ideas: Tools extend the reach and capacity of our hands.

The learning goals included in this activity are promoting understanding of the varieties and differences in tools that have been designed to make our work easier; appreciating human inventiveness in the creation of tools; increasing awareness that tools are energy driven; increasing skill in making thoughtful, intelligent comparisons based on data; increasing skill in suggesting reasoned hypotheses; increasing skill in raising intelligent questions that lead to information gathering.

This activity asks children to use the higher-order thinking skills of observing and comparing; classifying; suggesting hypotheses; imagining; examining assumptions; designing investigations; evaluating and judging.

Materials needed: An assortment of many different kinds of tools (hammer, saw, pliers, screwdriver, nails, scissors, paper punch, stapler, eggbeater, ruler, thermometer, scale, flashlight, mousetrap, needle, eraser, paper clips, air pump, magnet, wheels from a toy car or bicycle, fork, spoon).

Activity Card

Use the materials in the center to make some studies of tools.
   How do these tools work? How can you describe how they work?
   How do we use tools to work for us? How can you describe this?
   What observations have you made?

Sample Debriefing Questions to Follow the Play Activity

Asking children to reflect on their observations:

- What observations did you make about these tools?
- What observations did you make about how the tools work?
- What observations did you make about how tools help us do our work?
- What observations did you make about how tools make our work easier?
- What are your ideas about that?

Challenging children to think beyond their observations:

- How come it's easier to dig a hole with a shovel than with your hands? What are your ideas about that?
- How come it's easier to drive a nail into a piece of wood with a hammer than with a screw driver? What are your ideas about that?
- How do you suppose hammers (saws, scissors) got invented? What are your ideas?
- How are rulers and clocks alike? How are they different?

- What are tools for? What are your ideas about that?
- What kind of tool would you invent to write with in outer space?

Suggestions for Replay

Since there is more to be mined from the original activity card and tools, the children may replay productively with them for several additional sessions.

New tools (microscope, candles, thread, wire, ballpoint pens, plastic sheeting, buckets, straws, ice pick, barometer, telescope, magnifying lens, stethoscope, cell phone, atomizer, pocket calculator, tablet, laptop computer, camera) may be added to the center for use with the following types of new activity cards:

Conduct some investigations to see how a microscope works. What observations did you make? What do you suppose are some good uses for microscopes?

Classify the tools in the center. Arrange them into groups and give each group a name.

The children may carry out investigations in which they compare tools, such as a knife and a saw, a clock and a liquid measuring container. They may also take tools apart and study their working parts. As an additional activity, they may gather data about all the tools used in class, in the school, at home, or in a workplace.

Suggestions for More Creative Play

1. Writing poems or stories about the invention of a particular tool; about life without certain tools; about how we depend on tools; about topics of their own choosing.
2. Participating in arts and crafts projects such as designing and building tools; drawing pictures of tools important in their lives; inventing tools that have never been heard of before.
3. Dramatizing the discovery of a new tool that could, for example, transport you back in time, turn you invisible, or clean up your room.
4. Creating a play about the day that early people created the first wheel.

6. PLAYING WITH OUR OWN EYES, EARS, NOSES, AND TONGUES

Notes to teachers: This is a good activity to raise awareness that differences among students do not indicate their value. In other words, use this activity to enable children to appreciate that differences are differences; we can be different without being better or worse.

Big ideas: Our senses are used to gather and respond to information about our world. They also alert us to danger and keep us safe.

The learning goals include promoting awareness of specific sense organs, their distinguishing characteristics, and how they work; appreciation of individual differences without making value judgments; increasing skill in making thoughtful observations about how our senses work for us; raising intelligent questions; making comparisons of significant attributes; formulating reasonable hypotheses.

This activity asks children to use the higher-order thinking skills of observing, comparing, and classifying data; imagining and inventing; suggesting hypotheses; designing investigations; making decisions; evaluating and judging.

Materials needed: Small hand and magnifying mirrors, ceramic or plastic models of eyes or ears, tongue depressors, large magnifying glasses, flashlights.

Activity Card

Use the materials in this center to find out what you can about your eyes, ears, nose, and tongue. Make sure you don't put anything harmful near them.

Make some observations of your eyes. Study your eyes. Then compare them with the eyes of others in your group.

Make some observations of your ears. Study your ears. Then compare them with the ears of others in your group.

Make some observations of your nose. Study your nose. Then compare it with the noses of others in your group.

Make some observations of your tongue. Study your tongue. Then compare it with the tongues of others in your group.

Sample Debriefing Questions to Follow the Play Activity

Asking children to reflect on their observations:

- What observations did you make about your eyes? How are the eyes of the other children different? How are they alike? What did you observe about how eyes work?
- What observations did you make about your own ears? How are ears of the other children alike? How are they different?

- What observations did you make about your nose? How are noses of the others alike? How are they different?
- What observations did you make about your tongue? How are tongues of others alike? How are they different?

Challenging children to think beyond their observations:

- How come some eyes see better than others? How do you explain this?
- How do ears work? What are your ideas? How come some ears hear better than others? How do you explain this?
- How do noses work? What are your ideas?
- Why do you suppose the sense of smell (hearing, vision, taste) is so important? What are your ideas?
- What do you suppose impairs our vision (hearing, sense of smell)? What are your ideas about this?
- What do you suppose is the work of the tongue? What are your ideas?
- How does the tongue help us taste our food? What do you think?
- How come some cats and dogs can hear and smell better than humans? How do you explain this?
- How come some people judge others by the way they look? What do you suppose accounts for those judgments? Where do you suppose those ideas come from?
- How do we teach ourselves to be more accepting of individual differences, to respect the differences among us? What are your ideas about that?

Suggestions for Replay

Children may continue with investigations with the original activity card for several additional sessions. Additional insights can be gained when the makeup of the group changes.

Other activity cards such as the following may be added that shift the investigations onto a new plane:

- What are some things the eyes can do? Conduct some investigations and see what you can find out. Be very careful *not* to do anything that will harm your eyes.
- What are some things the ears can do? Conduct some investigations and see what you can find out. Be very careful *not* to do anything that will harm your ears.

- What are some things that noses can do? Conduct some investigations and see what you can find out. Be very careful *not* to do anything that will harm your nose.
- How do our tongues help us to speak? How does this work? See what you can find out.

Children may classify the eyes of all the children in the class. They may be asked to design investigations to see whose sense of hearing is more accurate.

Suggestions for More Creative Play

1. Writing poems or stories or telling stories that relate to sensory experiences on suggested topics (The boy or girl who could hear everything; The boy or girl who could not hear; The boy or girl who was super sensitive to loud noises), or other topics of the children's choosing.
2. Making pictures or building models of eyes, ears, noses, or tongues.
3. Participating in musical projects that involve studying sounds that are pleasurable and sounds that are harsh; listening for differences in pitch; singing in harmony.

7. PLAYING WITH HUMAN SKIN: A SENSE ORGAN

Notes to teachers: This is a good activity for children to appreciate that differences in skin pigmentation do not indicate their value. In other words, use this activity to enable children to appreciate that differences are differences; we can be different without being better or worse.

Big ideas: Our skin is a sense organ through which we take in information and which protects us.

The learning goals included are promoting awareness of and appreciation for the function of the skin as an outer protective covering and as a means through which we experience sensation; promoting awareness of how and what we learn from the sense of touch.

This activity asks children to use the higher-order thinking skills of observing and comparing; interpreting; suggesting hypotheses; examining assumptions; imagining and inventing; evaluating and judging; designing investigations; making decisions.

Materials needed: Magnifying lenses, small hand mirrors, thermometers, ice cubes, soft fabrics (velvet, silk, cotton), rough-textured fabrics (corduroy, brocade, Velcro), an assortment of objects that lend themselves to different tactile sensations (steel wool, metal, felt, sandpaper, chalk, clay, paste or glue, wooden and metal objects of rough and smooth textures, paper), cloths for blindfolds.

Activity Card

Use the materials in this center to find out what you can about what can be felt through touch.

Make some observations of what your skin can feel when your eyes are closed.

Talk to each other about the "messages" your skin sends to your brain.

What parts of your skin can feel things better than other parts? How do you know?

Conduct some investigations to discover how and what you can learn through the sense of touch.

Sample Debriefing Questions to Follow the Play Activity

Asking children to reflect on their observations:

- What observations did you make about your skin? About its texture? Its color? Its hair? Its temperature? About what your skin can feel?
- When your eyes are closed, how does touching an object give you information about it? What are your ideas?
- What information can you gather by touching? How do you know this?

Challenging children to think beyond their observations:

- How does skin tell the difference between hot and cold? How can you explain this?
- What is our skin for? What are your thoughts about this?
- How is our skin different from animal skin? What do you think?
- How come some parts of our skin have hair? What's the hair for? What hypotheses can you suggest to explain why we have hair on our skin?
- How come skins come in different colors? How do you explain this?
- How come some people consider certain skin colors better or worse than other colors? How can you explain that?
- How come some skins have freckles? Where do you suppose freckles come from?
- How come some skins are ticklish? What hypotheses can you suggest?

Suggestions for Replay

The original activity card will provide for many additional investigations in replay, and children should be encouraged to repeat and carry out new inquiries with the original materials.

New materials may be added for more challenging observations and investigations: a variety of other skins, such as fruit skins (apple, banana, orange, coconut, melon), vegetable skins (onion, potato, eggplant, squash), nut skins (almond shells, sunflower seed hulls), animal skins (pieces of leather and fur, molted reptile skins); small knives and microscopes if available. These materials should be used in conjunction with the following activity card:

> Conduct some investigations and make some observations about fruit (vegetable, animal) skins.
> How are fruit (vegetable, animal) skins different from human skins? How are they alike?
> Find as many similarities and differences as you can.

The children may be asked to design experiments with the use of the following new activity card:

> Design an investigation that would show how your skin can change its temperature.

Suggestions for More Creative Play

1. Drawing pictures of different skins (snake skins, alligator skins).
2. Finger painting.
3. Making fingerprints and comparing them.
4. Writing poems about skin.
5. Writing stories about the way we use the word *skin* idiomatically (He gets under my skin; She's got a thin/thick skin; It made my skin crawl; A skin as smooth as glass).

8. PLAYING WITH HIGH TECH

Note to teachers: This activity requires some IT materials, some of which may not be available for school use. Not every item on the materials list is necessary; in fact, if only a few tablets are available, that would work as well.

Big ideas: Technology has become an increasingly important part of our lives. We depend on technology for communication, for recreation, for work, for transportation, and for fun. Some high-tech devices make our work easier and faster.

The learning goals for this activity include promoting awareness of the many ways technology has impacted our lives and how much we depend on it.

This activity asks children to use the higher-order thinking skills of observing and comparing; classifying; suggesting hypotheses; examining assumptions; imagining and inventing; evaluating and judging; designing investigations.

Materials needed: Desktop computer, laptop computer, tablet computers, cell phones, instax cameras, switch light, Pixicade kit, robot toys, drones, remote controls, a variety of stuffed animals.

Activity Card

Play with these materials and see if you can make some observations about how important technology has become in our lives.

What are some uses of desktop or laptop computers? What are your ideas about this?

What are some uses of cell phones? What are your ideas about this?

How are robot toys different from stuffed animal toys? How are they alike?

How do we use tablets to entertain us? What are your ideas about this?

How are drones different from paper airplanes? How are they alike?

Sample Debriefing Questions to Follow the Play Activity

Asking children to reflect on their observations:

- What observations did you make about these high-tech devices? About how they are used? About how they are made?
- What differences did you observe about them? What similarities?
- What observations did you make about how important they are in our lives?
- What observations did you make about how they entertain us?

Challenging children to think beyond their observations:

- How important have high-tech devices become in your life? What examples can you give of how you use them?
- What did children do before they had tablets? What are your ideas about that?

- How does a computer (tablet, cell phone) make our lives easier or better? What are your ideas about this?
- Suppose you had to give up all of your high-tech toys. What would your life be like then? How would you describe it?
- Can a person get "stuck" on their tablet? Cell phone? How does this happen? What do you see as some consequences of that?

Suggestions for Replay

There should be many opportunities for children to play again with the high-tech devices since both individually and collectively they offer many options for exploration and examination.

Suggestions for More Creative Play

1. Drawing or painting pictures of some high-tech toys of the future.
2. Imagining what life would be like on a desert island without the use of high-tech tools and writing stories, poems, or plays about it.
3. Writing stories about a boy or girl who just got her or his first cell phone.
4. Writing a poem about a boy who couldn't stop playing games on his tablet.

CONCLUSION

While there are potentially dozens of other investigative play experiences that could be added to this group, the ones included above will doubtless give teachers and parents much to work with and many enjoyable hours of learning in the content area of science.

Chapter 11

Serious Players
Math

The curriculum area of math is a natural for children's play activities, since learning mathematical concepts is most successfully done with manipulative materials and through hands-on experiential play. Virtually all mathematical concepts lend themselves to such investigations: volume and capacity; shapes and sizes; symmetry; area; estimation and measurement of length, time, speed, temperature, and space; balance; angles.

Many examples are offered in this chapter to show how conceptual understanding may be developed in these areas. Creative play in mathematics may also occur in arts, crafts, music, and cooking activities. All of these types of activities are included in this section for playing with mathematics.

1. PLAYING WITH LIQUID VOLUME AND CAPACITY

Big ideas: The space filled remains unchanged, despite the differences in the shape of the container (principle of conservation). Volume refers to the amount of space in a hollow container.

The learning goals included in this activity are promoting understanding of the concept of conservation; promoting awareness that visual assessment of size and volume are not necessarily congruent with capacity.

This activity asks children to use the higher-order thinking skills of observing, comparing, and interpreting data; designing investigations; suggesting hypotheses; examining assumptions; applying principles to new situations.

Materials needed: Beakers of various sizes and shapes. (In order for the concept of conservation to be adequately examined, it is important to include several differently shaped containers that hold the same amount of liquid.) Also plastic containers, measuring cups, a water table or a large dishpan of water, paper towels, newspaper.

Activity Card

Use the materials to conduct some investigations about how much water it takes to fill containers of different sizes and shapes.

What did you observe about the amount of water it takes to fill the tall, skinny container?

What did you observe about the amount of water it takes to fill the short, fat container?

What did you observe about the amount of water it takes to fill the _____ container?

Talk together about your observations.

Sample Debriefing Questions to Follow the Play Activity

Asking children to reflect on their observations:

- What observations did you make about the amount of water it takes to fill the tall, skinny container?
- What observations did you make about the amount of water it takes to fill the short, fat container?
- How do you explain this? How is it possible that these two differently shaped containers hold the same amount of water? What are your ideas?
- If both of these containers (the short, fat and the tall, skinny) were filled with chocolate milk, which one would you want? How come?

Challenging children to think beyond their observations:

- How can you tell which container holds more water? How would you go about finding this out?
- How can you tell which container holds less water? How would you go about finding this out?
- How can you tell which containers hold the same amount of water? How would you find this out?
- How can you tell which container in the store holds more milk? Ice cream? Soda pop? Yogurt? What are your ideas?

Suggestions for Replay

Allowing for many more playful investigations with the original materials is a good idea before adding new materials or new activity cards.

In later replays, new containers of various sizes and shapes may be added, as well as new "pourable" substances for filling the containers. For example, sand, colored water, and small, solid objects (pebbles, marbles, buttons, paper clips, rubber bands, macaroni). These materials may be used in conjunction with the following activity cards:

- Use the materials to conduct some more investigations about how much sand (marbles, macaroni) it takes to fill containers of different sizes.
- Use the materials to conduct some investigations to find out how many marbles (pebbles, paper clips) it takes to fill containers of different sizes.
- Use the materials to conduct some investigations to find out which containers hold more (or less) water, sand, marbles, buttons. What observations have you made about the relationship between the shape of the container and its volume?

Suggestions for More Creative Play

1. Using paper and cardboard to make containers that hold the same amount of water (sand, rods, cubes, dominoes).
2. Figuring out a way to determine how much water it takes to fill up something with a very large volume (a swimming pool, an aquarium, a bathtub).
3. Designing containers to hold articles with irregular shapes (a two-hundred-pound octopus, a baby elephant, a slithery python, a giant helping of spaghetti).

2. PLAYING WITH DRY VOLUME AND CAPACITY

Big ideas: The space filled remains unchanged despite the differences in the shape of a container (principle of conservation). Volume refers to the amount of space in a container. The more volume, the greater the capacity.

The learning goals included in this activity are promoting understanding of the concept of conservation; promoting awareness that visual assessment of size and volume are not necessarily congruent with the actual volume.

This activity asks children to use the higher-order thinking skills of observing and comparing data; suggesting hypotheses; examining assumptions; designing investigations; applying principles to new situations.

Materials needed: Boxes of various sizes and shapes (shoe boxes, candy boxes, cookie boxes, mailing cartons, stationery boxes); one-square-inch plastic or wooden cubes. (For the principle of conservation to be adequately explored, it's important that some boxes of different shapes are able to contain the same number of one-square-inch cubes.)

Activity Card

Use the material to conduct some investigations about how many blocks it takes to fill containers of different sizes and shapes.

What do you observe about how many blocks it takes to fill the long, narrow box?

What do you observe about how many blocks it takes to fill the short, fat box?

What do you observe about the number of blocks it takes to fill the _____ box?

Talk together about your observations.

Sample Debriefing Questions to Follow the Play Activity

Asking children to reflect on their observations:

- What observations did you make about how many blocks it takes to fill the long, narrow box?
- What observations did you make about how many blocks it takes to fill the short, fat box?
- How do you explain this? How come these two different shaped boxes hold the same number of blocks? What are your ideas?
- Suppose you tried to fill these boxes with chocolates. How many chocolates would fill the short, fat box? How many would fill the long, narrow box? How did you figure that out? What assumptions have you made about the chocolates?
- If both of these boxes (short and fat, long and narrow) were filled with cookies, which one would you want? How come? What assumptions have you made about the cookies?

Challenging children to think beyond their observations:

- When you look at these boxes, how can you tell which one will hold more? What are your ideas about that? What assumptions have you made?
- How can you tell which one will hold less? What are your ideas about that?
- How could you tell which boxes hold the same amount? What do you think? What assumptions have you made?

- How can you tell which box on the shelf in the market holds more cookies? Candy? Marbles? Cereal? Pencils? What are your ideas about that?
- How come your eyes tell you that something is true, but when you do your experiment, you find out that it is not true? How do you explain it?

Suggestions for Replay

Replay with the same materials and the same activity card should be allowed to continue for several more sessions, since the children are likely to find many new ways to investigate these concepts.

New and different shaped containers, including some with odd shapes, may be added for later replay sessions, as well as new materials for filling the boxes (Cuisenaire rods, dominoes, building blocks, Lego, and materials of different shapes such as diamonds, hexagons, octagons, rounds). These may be used with the following activity cards:

- Use the materials to conduct some more investigations about how many blocks (dominoes, rods) it takes to fill boxes of different shapes and sizes.
- Use the materials to conduct some more investigations to find out how many diamonds (hexagons, octagons) it takes to fill boxes of different sizes.
- Use the materials to conduct some investigations to find out which boxes hold more (or fewer) dominoes (cubes, blocks, hexagons). What observations have you made about the relationship between the shape of a box and its volume?

Suggestions for More Creative Play

1. Cooking (popcorn, cookies, muffins, jello); making butter.
2. Making boxes with cardboard or construction paper.
3. Building with blocks (Keva blocks, dominoes, one-inch blocks, Cuisenaire rods, Lego).

3. PLAYING WITH SHAPES AND SIZES

Big ideas: Some shapes, such as a square, triangle, rectangle, and diamond, can be used to cover a surface without leaving a gap or overlapping. Two lines coming together at a point form an angle.

The learning goals for this activity include promoting awareness of the differences among the two-dimensional shapes of squares, triangles, and rectangles; promoting understanding of the concept of "fit without leaving a gap"; developing awareness of the concept of angles.

This activity asks children to use the higher-order thinking skills of observing, comparing, classifying, and interpreting data; designing investigations; applying principles to new situations.

Materials needed: Cut-out cardboard shapes of different sizes and colors (rectangles, squares, diamonds, triangles); if available, attribute blocks; large sheets of graph paper; rulers or meter sticks; scissors and pencils.

Activity Card

Use the materials to make some observations of how these differently shaped pieces fit when you arrange them on a piece of graph paper.

What observations can you make about how the squares fit? The rectangles? The triangles? The diamonds?

Try to arrange the different shapes on the graph paper so that they fit without leaving a gap. Talk together about your observations.

Sample Debriefing Questions to Follow the Play Activity

Asking children to reflect on their observations:

- What observations did you make about how the squares fit? Rectangles? Triangles? Diamonds?
- How are squares like rectangles? How are they different?
- How are triangles like diamonds? How are they different?
- In what ways are the squares (rectangles, triangles) alike? In what ways are they different?
- What observations did you make about how different shapes fit together without leaving a gap?

Challenging children to think beyond their observations:

- How can you describe a square (rectangle, triangle, diamond)? What kind of shape does it have?
- What observations did you make about the sides of these figures? About their corners?
- In what ways are the corners (angles) of the squares, rectangles, and triangles alike? How are they different?
- What other things in the room can you observe that have similar kinds of corners as squares and triangles? How can you tell they are similar?

Suggestions for Replay

Replay with the same materials and the original activity card can continue for several additional sessions, since these materials should lead to several new investigations.

In subsequent replays, new shapes (hexagons, octagons, pentagons, circles, and half circles) may be added, in conjunction with new activity cards. For example:

- Use the materials to make a design with squares (rectangles, triangles, diamonds) on the graph paper. What observations did you make about how the squares fit together? The rectangles? The diamonds?
- Use the circles and half circles to make a design on the graph paper. What observations did you make about how the circles fit together? The half circles?
- Use the octagons (pentagons, hexagons) to make a design on the graph paper. What observations did you make about how the octagons (pentagons, hexagons) fit together?

Suggestions for More Creative Play

1. Design three doghouses, the first using only squares, the second using only triangles, the third using only octagons.
2. Work with a partner, look everywhere in the room to find objects containing triangular, rectangular, and square shapes. Draw some pictures of what has been found.
3. Create designs using only diamond shapes.
4. Design and cut out five different shapes that are unlike any of the above shapes. Give each new shape a name.

4. PLAYING WITH AREA AND PERIMETER

Big ideas: The surface included within a set of lines is the area. The area of a surface is different from its boundary or perimeter. If you want to enclose a region, you need to figure out its perimeter. If you want to cover the surface, you need to figure out the area.

The learning goals for this activity include: to promote understanding of the concept of area, that is, the amount required to cover a surface; to differentiate between the concepts of area and perimeter; and to develop skill in solving problems requiring the calculation of area.

This activity asks children to use the higher-order thinking skills of observing, comparing, and interpreting data; suggesting hypotheses; examining assumptions; designing projects and investigations.

Materials needed: Large sheets of graph paper, cut into differently sized squares and rectangles; large pieces of graph paper cut into irregular shapes; multicolored one-inch square pieces of cardboard; rulers and scissors; rope or string.

Activity Card

Use the materials to conduct some investigations about the size of the surface of the squares, rectangles, and other shapes. Use the materials to conduct some investigations about the perimeters of (the distance around) these pieces.

What observations can you make about how many colored squares it takes to cover the large piece of graph paper?

What observations can you make about how many colored squares it takes to cover the smaller piece of graph paper?

What surfaces need more colored squares to cover them? Which are the same? What observations did you make?

What observations did you make about measuring the perimeters of (the distance around) these pieces of paper?

What did you observe about the difference between areas and perimeters?

Sample Debriefing Questions to Follow the Play Activity

Asking children to reflect on their observations:

- What observations did you make about how many colored squares it took to cover the surface of a piece of graph paper?
- What observations did you make about the surfaces that needed more colored squares? Fewer colored squares?
- What observations did you make about the surfaces that needed the same number of colored squares to cover their surfaces?
- How did you figure out how to cover the odd-shaped surfaces? What ideas did you have?
- What are some good ways to measure the perimeter of (the distance around) the regular- and irregular-shaped papers? How did you figure that out?

Challenging children to think beyond their observations:

- When you look at the surfaces of the graph paper that has been cut into squares and rectangles, how can you tell which ones have the larger surface areas? What are your ideas about that?
- When you look at the irregularly shaped surfaces, how can you tell which ones have the larger (smaller) surface area? What are your ideas about that?
- If you wanted to cover a rectangle (square, irregularly shaped piece) with a carpet, how would you know which size carpet to get? How might this surface be measured? What do you think?
- How did you figure out the difference between the area of a surface and its perimeter? What are some good ways to make those measurements? What are your ideas about that?

Suggestions for Replay

Children should have many more opportunities to replay with the same graph paper, rectangles, squares, and irregularly shaped pieces, since many new inquiries can be carried out with the same materials.

In later replays, new shapes of graph paper (triangles, circles, half circles, hexagons) may be added in conjunction with the following new activity cards:

- Use the materials to conduct some investigations about the surface areas of these shapes.
- Use the materials to conduct investigations about the perimeters of these shapes.
- What are some good ways to measure surface areas and perimeters of irregularly shaped objects?
- Use the materials to figure how many squares it takes to cover the surface of a book, a piece of paper, a box top, a desktop, an envelope, a tennis ball.
- Place graph paper on the floor and draw around a shoe of everyone in the group.
  Which shoe covers the largest surface area?
  Which shoe covers the smallest area?
  Which has the largest and smallest perimeter?
  Figure out a way to calculate the areas and perimeters of each of the shoes.

Suggestions for More Creative Play

1. Creating and inventing ways to figure out the surface area and perimeters of leaves, hand shapes, animal shapes, and the outside surfaces of boxes, coffee cans, soup cans.
2. Creating and designing shapes with a given (fixed) surface area, for example, a shape that has an area of nine square inches that would be a good shape for a duck pond.
3. Designing or creating space of certain specifications to plant a garden, build a giant chessboard, design a maze, design a kite.
4. Figuring out ways to measure the surface area of a puddle, a ball, a balloon, a totem pole.

5. PLAYING WITH LINEAR MEASUREMENT

Big ideas: Linear dimensions of objects can be measured; standards units of measure are agreed upon by common consent; they help us to understand and communicate what we mean.

The learning goals for this activity include promoting awareness of the value of communicating to each other in quantifiable terms that others can understand; promoting increased skill in using standard units of measure.

This activity asks children to use the higher-order thinking skills of observing, comparing, classifying, and interpreting data; designing projects and investigations; imagining and creating; suggesting hypotheses; examining assumptions.

Materials needed: Tape measures, inch and centimeter rulers, yardsticks and metersticks, pieces of string or yarn, rubber bands, unit blocks, toothpicks, straws, large pieces of paper, scissors, pencils or felt pens.

Activity Card

Use the materials to make some observations about how objects can be measured.

What observations can you make about how to measure the top of your desk? The height of your desk? The height of the teacher's desk? The width of the classroom door? The height of the door? The width of the window?

What differences do you observe when you measure these objects with a ruler? A yardstick? A meterstick? A piece of string? Unit blocks? Rubber bands? Your feet?

Sample Debriefing Questions to Follow the Play Activity

Asking children to reflect on their observations:

- What observations did you make about how to measure the top of a desk? Height of a desk? A door? A window?
- What observations did you make when you measured these things with a ruler? A yardstick? A meterstick? A piece of string? Unit blocks? Toothpicks? Rubber bands? Your feet?
- Which is easier to use when you measure? What are your ideas?
- Why do you suppose we need to know the measurements of these objects? What are your ideas?

Challenging children to think beyond their observations:

- When a child measured the window, she found it was eighteen inches across. When another child measured the same window, he found it was twenty-three rubber bands across. What are some of your ideas about these two ways of measuring?
- When a child measured the length of the classroom with her feet, she found that it was seventy-four of her feet long. Then another child measured it with his feet. He found that it was eighty-six of his feet long. Why do you suppose people stopped using their feet as measuring tools? How do you explain this?
- Why do you suppose it helps us to use measurements that we can agree on? What do you see as some reasons for this?
- What happens when two people measuring the same distance or object disagree about the measurement? How should they resolve their argument? What are your ideas?

Suggestions for Replay

Replaying with the same measuring tools and objects for several additional sessions should lead to even more fruitful inquiries. In later replays, paper and scissors may be added with new activity cards to encourage new measuring investigations. For example:
 This activity requires at least two children.

- Use the paper to make a tracing of one of your own feet. Cut out your tracing.

- Use your foot tracings to measure the window, the door, the length of the room. How are your foot measurements alike? How are they different? How do you explain this?
  Then measure the window (door, etc.) with a ruler or yardstick.
  What observations can you make about the differences between these two ways of measuring?

- Use the materials to measure the height of every person in your group. Make a chart that shows the height of all the children in the group.

- What happens when two people measuring the same item disagree on its size? How do you explain how that happens? How do you suggest they resolve the differences?

Suggestions for More Creative Play

1. Creating and inventing ways to measure larger distances (from the floor to the ceiling; from home to school; from home to the shopping mall; from Alabama to Minnesota; from Newfoundland to the North Pole).
2. Creating and inventing ways to measure how high different balls bounce.
3. Creating and inventing ways to measure the amount of snow or rain fallen during a specific time period.
4. Creating and inventing ways to measure a puddle.
5. Writing a story about two adults who were arguing about the size of their gardens.
6. Writing a story about the day that the first tool for making accurate measurements was invented.

6. PLAYING WITH COUNTING

Big ideas: Number is an attribute that represents a set of objects; numerals are names of numbers; counting is a way of determining more, less, the same, how many.

The learning goals included in this activity are providing opportunities to explore mathematical relationships in combining and removing sets and subsets; determining how many; examining the concepts of more, less, the same.

This activity asks children to use the higher-order thinking skills of observing, comparing, and classifying data; suggesting hypotheses; examining assumptions; interpreting data; designing projects and investigations; creating and imagining.

Serious Players

Materials needed: Cuisenaire rods or other counting rods, cubical counting blocks, other "counters" such as buttons, spools, dominoes, discs, small stones, toothpicks; about one dozen cut-out circles of colored cardboard or colored paper in different diameters. The counting objects can be varied, as can the colored circles, so investigative play with counting has extensive permutations with even these initial materials.

Activity Card

Use the materials to make some observations about numbers. How many Cuisenaire rods can you fit onto the red circle? How many rods can you fit onto the orange circle? Which can hold more rods? Which holds less?

How many buttons can you fit onto the green circle? How many buttons can you fit onto the yellow circle? Which circle holds more buttons? Which holds less?

What observations can you make about the number of stones, toothpicks, dominoes, buttons that can fit onto any of the colored circles?

Sample Debriefing Questions to Follow the Play Activity

Asking children to reflect on their observations:

- What observations did you make about how many buttons (stones, rods) fit on different circles?
- What observations did you make about which circles hold more items? Which hold less? What did these investigations tell you about numbers?

Challenging children to think beyond their observations:

- How come the orange circle holds more stones but fewer buttons? How do you explain this?
- What do you think? Will the blue circle will hold more stones or buttons? What is your estimation?
- Which colored circles hold exactly eight (or nine, ten, seven) buttons (dominoes, stones)? What is your estimation?
- Which two colored circles together hold nine (or ten, eight, seven) buttons (dominoes, stones, unit blocks)? What's your estimation?
- If someone tells you that he is eight years old, what does that mean to you? What are your ideas?

Suggestions for Replay

Since there are so many possibilities using combinations of colored circles and counters, replay with the original materials and activity card might carry on for several days. Children should be encouraged to carry out extensive investigations with these materials.

When they are ready to move on, new colored circles of larger sizes and new objects for "counters" (toy cars, thumb tacks, paper clips, crayons, popcorn) may be added. These additional materials are used in conjunction with the following activity cards:

Use the counters to figure out an answer to these questions:

- How many toy cars would you need to give everyone in the class two cars?
- How could you record this information to show how you got that number?

Use the counters to figure out an answer to these questions:

- How many cookies would you need to give everyone in the class three cookies?
- How could you record this information to show how you got that number?

Suggestions for More Creative Play

1. Playing store, with real coins (one hundred pennies can go a long way), toy cash drawer, play money.
2. Playing games in which counting or keeping score is used (ten pins, dominoes, dice, ball games).
3. Singing number songs ("This Old Man," "Sing a Song of Sixpence," "Five Little Chickadees," "One, Two, Buckle My Shoe").
4. Cooking or baking and sharing out cookies, muffins, popcorn.
5. Drawing figures to illustrate a "number sentence" ($3 + 4 = 7$; $7 - 3 = 4$).
6. Planning, budgeting, and shopping for ingredients to make applesauce, pancakes, butter, strawberry shortcake.

7. PLAYING WITH TIME

Big ideas: The passage of time can be measured. There are standards units of measure for hours and minutes, days, months, and years. Our standard units of time are measured by the rotation of the earth around the sun.

The learning goals for this activity include providing opportunities for experiences with standard units for measuring time; increasing appreciation for the usefulness of standard units of measure in communicating our thoughts to others; promoting awareness of what can be done in different time periods.

This activity asks children to use the higher-order thinking skills of observing, comparing, and interpreting data; designing projects and investigations; creating and inventing; suggesting hypotheses; examining assumptions.

Materials needed: A variety of instruments that measure hours, minutes and days—for example, an hourglass, clocks (analog, digital, windup, alarm, sweep second hand, wall clock), timers, and a stopwatch; cardboard clock with movable minute and second hands.

Activity Card

Use the materials to make some studies of time.

How is time measured? What kinds of instruments measure time?

How do clocks measure time? How are clocks and timers alike? How are they different?

Do some playing around with the time devices and see what observations you can make.

Sample Debriefing Questions to Follow the Play Activity

Asking children to reflect on their observations

- What observations did you make about how clocks measure time?
- What observations did you make about how timers measure time?
- What are some differences between digital clocks and analog clocks? What are some similarities?
- What's a minute? A second? An hour? How are these measured? What are your ideas?

Challenging children to think beyond their observations:

- How long do you suppose it takes to jump one hundred times? What's your estimate?
- How long do you suppose it takes to drink a glass of water? What's your estimate?
- Does it take longer to read a book or eat an apple? What do you think? How do you know that is true?
- Why do you suppose we need to measure time? What's good about being able to do that?

- What assumptions do you make when you estimate how long it takes to walk home from school?
- How are estimations different from the actual measurement of the time?
- What do you suppose people mean when they say, "Time flies"? What are your ideas?

Suggestions for Replay

New activity cards may be added that involve different kinds of calculations with time. Children may begin by estimating the amount of time and then measuring the time:

How long would it take to bounce a ball one hundred times? Blow up a balloon? Fill a gallon bucket with water? Eat lunch? Fly a kite? Walk home from school? Train your dog to fetch a ball? Play a video game?

New materials may be added for children to measure days, weeks, months, years. Different kinds of calendars (day, week, month) may be used in conjunction with the following new activity cards:

- Make some observations of the clock and the calendar. How are these time measures alike? How are they different?
- Make some observations about how calendars measure time. How are the days, weeks, months measured?
- Use the calendars to figure out some ways of measuring how long each person in a group will have to wait until his or her birthday. Make a chart to record your findings.

Other replay activities may involve gathering and classifying time schedules (TV schedules, airplane/train/bus schedules); keeping records of everyone's birthday; calculating how long it takes different children to walk to school every day; designing investigations to determine the time at which the sun sets every day in the month of January and in the month of May.

Suggestions for More Creative Play

1. Making a clock, a sundial, an hourglass, the calendar month of a child's birthday.
2. Inventing ways to figure out how much time it takes for a bird to fly from a nest into the air, a balloon to release its air, a leaf to fall to the ground.
3. Engaging in dramatic play on time themes (I hate to wait for my mother to finish her shopping! I hate to go to bed at 9:00! I hate to have only

fifteen minutes for recess! I hate to have to wait for my brother to finish his cereal!).
4. Writing stories or poems about "when time flies."
5. Writing stories of poems about "when time stands still."
6. Making an illustration of how you think the atomic clock on the wall is able to change by itself from daylight saving time to standard time.

Conclusion

These curriculum activities for serious play with math concepts represent only a fraction of what is possible. They are, of course, suitable for school as well as for intrepid parents at home with minor modifications. In either case, they should lead to many rich and exciting playful investigations in which children's concept development in mathematics is enhanced. They may, of course, serve as examples for other serious plays in mathematics.

Chapter 12

Serious Players
Moral and Ethical Dilemmas

The ability to put oneself in another's shoes is called "empathy." Empathy is not a trait we are born with; it is a developed skill learned best by the examples of significant adults—parents, teachers, and others who demonstrate empathy in their day-to-day dealings with children and other adults. Through such exposure, children learn intuitively and by example the ways to behave with others. In the absence of such exemplars, it may be taught with the application of some consistent and effective strategies (Carkhuff 1969; Gordon 2012).

In either case, empathic understanding is, not to exaggerate, the basis for building respectful, caring, and positive human relationships. The absence of empathy leaves a huge deficit in our relationships with others—children and adults. It leaves us open to false judgment, to prejudice, to contempt, and in worse-case scenarios to aggression and violence. We cannot "act out" with harm if we are "in tune" with another person; our empathy implicitly prohibits such behavior. We are more inclined to help, not hurt.

One cannot develop empathy without a sense of one's personal power. Those with acute power deficits cannot respond with empathy to others. Their power needs preclude such humanistic responses to others. The two conditions—a sense of one's own personal power and the ability to be empathic reside as two parts of an integrated whole person.

Since the development of personal power through allowing children choices and respecting those choices has been addressed substantively in earlier chapters of this book, this chapter will focus primarily on the development of empathy during the early childhood years. Teaching children to become more empathic follows the play-debrief-replay framework described in earlier chapters. The significant difference is that the play activities are more in the realm of "minds on" rather than "hands on."

PLAYING WITH INFORMED DECISION MAKING AND GOOD JUDGMENT

Chapters 7–11 in this book include a large number of suggestions for investigative play activities that build children's conceptual understanding in several areas of the curriculum, extend their knowledge in those areas, and promote self-respect, personal power, and critical thinking through the instructional framework called play-debrief-replay.

In this chapter, strategies for playing with ideas are presented as ways to inform children's decision making, guiding them through critical examination so that they may make better decisions about "the right thing to do." These mind-stretching activities begin with the obvious—children's literature.

Teachers and parents will not be new to using written narratives to present children with multifaceted dilemmas. There are literally hundreds of children's stories that fill this role (a list of a few is included later in this chapter). Playing with ideas takes a somewhat different form than what was found in the "hands-on" activities in the earlier chapters.

These plays begin with reading aloud the selected story to the children. Because children are so easily immersed in stories, their active engagement occurs naturally. Many children can actually "live" the story in their minds as it is read. Stretching minds, promoting the development of informed decision making and good judgment, occurs during the debriefing stage of the process. As seen in the investigative plays in earlier chapters, effective debriefing is strengthened by the preparation of questions that stimulate thinking about the issues.

DEBRIEFING

All of the conditions of debriefing described in chapter 6 are applicable here. The skill of attending, for example—listening closely to what the child is saying—is the bedrock of the debriefing process. It requires the ability to hear not only the words but also the nuances of expression, discerning deeper and unstated meanings. It involves picking up on the kinds of feelings underlying the statements, hearing and comprehending the "fullness" of what is being said. It also means freeing oneself from the desire to comment on or judge the statements.

Such skills may come more easily in debriefing investigative play, where children are exploring bubbles or number sets or consonant blends—activities in which the content doesn't create tension between moral positions of right and wrong. There are few personal biases that may influence an adult's response in the investigation of bubbles. But when the responses lie in the moral/ethical arena, where personal preference, bias, values, and beliefs are being heatedly debated, it is more difficult for the adult to assume that neutral stance and allow children the freedom to state their own views without judgmental comment. How does a teacher or parent learn to remain neutral?

Unfortunately, there is no short course, no single correct way to do this. But an effective approach lies in developing one's own ability to learn to listen to oneself critically during the debriefing process. Using either video or audio playback adds a clinical perspective and allows for more detailed study of one's responses in a context removed from the actual event. Studying closely the way the discussion has unfolded, reflecting nondefensively on when neutrality has been maintained and in what situations it has been lost, the adult gains insight into the steps to be taken in the next debriefing session.

Like other developmental growth skills, this incremental process is slow and may be a little painful, but within it lie the keys to the adult's professional growth as an effective discussion leader.

This is not to say that a teacher or parent never gives an opinion, states a bias, tells a child what they think is "right." While not effective as a strategy that builds thoughtful reflection, adults' opinions reveal their values. Teachers and parents are the moral exemplars for children and should, selectively and appropriately, tell children what they think, what they believe, what values they hold dear. From such disclosures, children learn about the values of people they respect, and the importance of such learning should not be underestimated.

But teachers' and parents' revelations about personal values do not occur during debriefing, lest they influence the children's ideas and make them give the adult just what he or she wants to hear. This has the effect of making the debriefing the discussion leader's game and preventing children from thinking through the reasons for their own moral positions.

Paraphrasing, asking questions that require analysis, and asking questions that challenge thinking are all part and parcel of debriefing centered on problems with moral and ethical dimensions. Questions used, of course, are all of the "higher order" kind and allow for many points of view. They avoid calling for "right answers" since the discussion is centered more on what the children think than it is on knowing answers.

In leading the debriefing, the discussion leader will want to ensure that all points of view are heard and respected, that children feel safe about offering their opinions, and that they do not subtly "angle" for a particular resolution. For a successful debriefing, it is imperative that children be allowed to express their own opinions without being influenced by the discussion leader's thoughts on "the right thing to do."

In debriefing stories where moral dilemmas and ethical issues are involved, these contentious issues are more productively examined when debriefing questions follow a hierarchy that begins with the examination of data and moves through the analysis of that data, to the identification of values issues, and finally to determining actions. In this intellectually healthy process, children develop intelligent habits of the mind, in which suggestions for action are informed by thoughtful consideration of data, rather than by impulsive bursts of "off the cuff" suggestions.

Initially, young children will likely approach such discussions from quite naïve perspectives. Perhaps moral admonitions will be proposed, such as "She should be good to her sister" or "They should try to get along." Very likely solutions will be offered before the data have been examined and analyzed. But after time, and in the presence of questions that call for looking beyond the surface and digging for deeper meanings, children grow in their critical skills and learn the habits of intelligent thinking in the same way they learn to read—through exposure and experience.

REPLAY

Replay activities follow debriefing in playing with ideas as they do in investigative play, since follow-up activities allow children opportunities to reexamine the situations, and the different points of view expressed in debriefing benefit from the perspective of time, coupled with ongoing reflection. Replay can take several forms, not limited to the following:

- Further discussion of issues in small groups
- Role-playing the story, with characters' feelings highlighted
- Further discussion of issues with individual and small groups of children
- Gathering data from other children about similar incidents in their lives
- Discussion of similar incidents from lived experiences
- Reading other stories with similar themes
- Creating stories with similar themes

CHILDREN'S BOOKS THAT EXAMINE MORAL/ETHICAL ISSUES

From classic fairy tales like "Cinderella," "Hansel and Gretel," and "Rapunzel" to more modern stories, a wealth of children's stories is available for examining issues with moral/ethical dimensions. Parents and teachers will have their own favorites, but for those who are new to this venue, particularly appropriate suggestions are include the following:

Brown, Margaret Wise. 1986. *The Dead Bird*. New York: HarperCollins.

Carlson, Nancy. 1990. *Annie and the New Kid*. New York: Viking.

Carroll, Jessica, and Craig Smith. 1995. *Billy the Punk*. Australia: Random House.

Heide, Florence. 1971. *The Shrinking of Treehorn*. New York: Holiday House.

Kellogg, Stephen. 1971. *Can I Keep Him?* New York: Dial.

Lasker, Joseph. 1974. *He's My Brother*. New York: Whitman.

Le Roy, Glen. 1981. *Lucky Stiff*. New York: McGraw Hill.

Levy, Elizabeth. 1979. *Nice Little Girls*. New York: Delacorte.

Mathieson, Feroza. 1988. *Lost at the Fair*. London: Black.

Mendez, Phil. 1989. *The Black Snowman*. New York: Scholastic.

Staples, Sarah. 1990. *Cordelia Dance*. New York: Dial.

Teague, Mark. 1989. *The Trouble with the Johnsons*. New York: Scholastic.

Viorst, Judith. 1978. *Alexander, Who Used to Be Rich Last Sunday*. New York: Macmillan.

Wells, Rosemary. 1973. *Noisy Nora*. New York: Dial.

———. 1981. *Timothy Goes to School*. New York: Dial.

———. 1991. *Fritz and the Mess Fairy*. New York: Dial.

Wilhelm, Hans. 1986. *Let's Be Friends Again*. New York: Crown.

Winthrop, Elizabeth. 1985. *Tough Eddie*. New York: Dutton.

A few books about social issues:

Bates, Amy, and Juniper Bates. 2018. *The Big Umbrella*. New York: Simon & Schuster.

Cain, Janan. 2021. *The Way I Feel*. Seattle: Parenting Press.

Choi, Yangsook. 2001. *The Name Jar*. New York: Knopf.

Couric, Katherine. 2000. *The Brand New Kid*. New York: Doubleday.

Estes, Eleanor. 1944. *The Hundred Dresses*. San Diego: Harcourt.

Fox, Mem (2006). *Whoever You Are*. New York: Houghton Mifflin.

Hale, Shannon, and LeUyen Pham. 2021. *Friends Forever*. New York: First Second.

Karst, Patrice, and Joanne Lew-Vriethoff. 2018. *The Invisible String*. Boston: Little, Brown.

Katz, Karen. 2002. *The Colors of Us.* New York: Square Fish.

Lester, Julius, and Karen Barbour. 2020. *Let's Talk About Race*. New York: HarperCollins.

Nagara, Innosanto. 2012. *A Is for Activist*. New York: Triangle Square.

Parr, Todd. 2009. *It's Okay to be Different*. Boston: Little, Brown.

Reynolds, Peter. 2003. *The Dot*. Sommerville, MA: Candlewick.

Sotomayor, Sonia, and Rafael Lopez. 2019. *Just Ask! Be Different, Be Brave, Be You*. New York: Philomel.

Woodson, Jacqueline, and E. B. Lewis. 2001. *The Other Side*. New York: Putnam.

There are also reference books that are treasuries of stories for children in a variety of areas that are particularly helpful in searching out what is available. School and public libraries and librarians are essential resources in recommending books.

In addition to children's books, films, TV programs, videos, toys, comic books, and DVDs are also useful resources for inquiring into critical questions of value, for example:

- What's the right thing to do?
- What's good about that?
- What do I think about that?
- What's important to me?

- What are the potential consequences of what I believe?
- What should be done about this?

Once teachers and parents have begun to investigate appropriate material for young children dealing with moral and ethical issues, the chances are great that what is available will extend far beyond the time available for such inquiries.

PLAYING WITH MORAL/ETHICAL ISSUES IN CONVERSATIONS

Big ideas: Being a good listener and responding to another with care and kindness is an essential feature of positive human relationships. The way we talk to and connect with each other is an important indicator of who we are.

Learning goals: To give students practice in listening and responding to others with kindness and care; to give students practice in observing and improving the way they interact with others.

The thinking skills incorporated in this activity are observing and comparing; evaluating; examining assumptions; interpreting.

Materials needed: A group of cards, each with a suggested topic for discussion. These topics may come from in class experiences or can be taken from this list: getting along together; friends; accepting other people's points of view; possessions; how it feels to be rejected; insistence on being right; a friend in trouble; a new child who doesn't speak English; getting even; calling names; tattling; discrimination; borrowing and not giving back; consequences of broken rules; breaking rules/laws; what's fair; dangerous play; getting into fights; settling arguments; punishments; stealing; cheating; to tell or not to tell; littering; consumerism; taking the blame; lies, honesty, truth telling; keeping a promise; the need to win or to be first; responsibility for the protection of the environment; playing tricks; keeping secrets; bowing to the pressure of the group; handling anger.

ACTIVITY CARD

Work in trios. One person chooses a topic to discuss; the second person responds by listening carefully to what is being said and by responding in a way that shows kindness and that you care. The third person is the observer, who listens and watches the way both are talking and responding to each other. After the conversation, the observer makes comments about what he or she has heard and seen and makes suggestions for how the responder might improve his or her responses.

Then change roles so that each has a turn to be the speaker, the responder, and the observer.

SAMPLE DEBRIEFING QUESTIONS TO FOLLOW THE PLAY ACTIVITY

Asking children to reflect on their observations:

- What observations did you make about the topics that were chosen by each of the speakers?
- What observations did you make about how the responder showed that she or he cared about what the speaker was saying?
- What observations did you make about how the responder showed kindness in his or her responses?
- What observations did you make about how the responder helped the speaker to say what was on his or her mind?
- What observations did you make about how the observer helped the responder to become more aware of how he or she was responding to the speaker?

Challenging children to think beyond their observations:

- How, in your view, did the responder help the speaker to feel safe about what he or she was saying? What did the responder say or do to make the speaker feel safe?
- How do you become a good listener? What do you think is necessary to do that?
- What do you need to do in order to make a speaker feel safe about telling you his or her ideas?
- How do good listening skills help us to be better friends to each other? What are your ideas about that?

SUGGESTIONS FOR REPLAY

Children should have many more opportunities to practice these listening and responding skills in trios that are ever changing.

SUGGESTIONS FOR MORE CREATIVE PLAY

1. Writing stories or dramas that focus on responding with kindness to others and why this is important in our human relationships.
2. Creating comic strips that show the way people behave toward each other unkindly or with disregard for their feelings.

CONCLUSION

Many of the play activities in this book have been focused primarily on the intellectual development of young children. This chapter shifts gears in focusing on their character development. It would not be an exaggeration to say that one without the other leaves children bereft. To be "clever" without being humane gives license to acts that can be brutal, savage, barbaric.

Early childhood is a gold mine of opportunity for children to learn to examine moral/ethical issues and to grow in their awareness and their understanding that reasons for their actions betray who they are and who they hope to become. These are the building blocks of character development and social responsibility. It is for teachers and parents of young children to mine that gold, to make the most of these opportunities that enable children to take important steps on the pathway to their growing morality.

SECTION III

Epilogue

Chapter 13

What's Important?

There has been much written in the news in the past months about the "loss in academic achievement" of students when schools were closed during the heightened anxiety about the spread of COVID. Despite students' access to online learning, reports focused on missed educational opportunities and concern about students' potential declining scores on standardized tests.

Although anxieties and concerns are real and should not be dismissed out of hand, the knee-jerk response to them is often to put pressure on students, teachers, and schools to "bear down" with instructional strategies that are aimed at "catching up" what has been lost or missed.

In some classrooms this means more intense concentration on academics, more homework, more time on task, more drill, less music and art, and certainly less play. In fact, in some kindergartens, emphasis is now on sitting quietly, doing workbook and worksheet exercises, rote learning of numbers and letters—the "stuff" that is usually found in first grade.

And in the face of all of that, here comes a book espousing the importance of play in the emotional and academic development of children. How does a teacher or parent know what is right? Which is the best course of action? How is a choice to be made between these two seemingly disconnected options?

THE DILEMMAS OF CHOOSING

How does a teacher or parent decide? What are some reasonable and responsible guidelines they might use in charting a course through the many ambiguities of decision making about appropriate curriculum content for students? As with all educational practice, it comes down to what each teacher or parent believes. What do teachers or parents have to believe about teaching, learning, and children to choose play as an essential component for learning? What beliefs would be antithetical to such a choice?

Teachers and parents who choose allowing much time for children to play—either with hands-on or "minds-on" tasks—have to believe first of all in the merit of play as an essential condition for the intellectual and emotional growth of children. This means that learning environments are not perceived as a place of silence where children sit quietly listening and watching the teacher telling and instructing, but rather places where children do the work, places where they talk to each other, discuss ideas, debate and argue, laugh, move about, and find the materials they need.

They are places where children spill water, knock over paint, break materials, tear plastic sheeting, and have all the accidents that occur when people work actively with materials. These teachers and parents must believe that active participation of children cannot occur without the "mess" that is a normal by-product of that kind of active engagement with material. An environment that allows for creative play is one in which the children's busyness and the noise connected with normal, healthy productivity are the order of the day.

Teachers choosing to incorporate creative and investigative play in their programs have to believe with Bettleheim (1987) that play is children's work and that children learn more, intellectually, socially, and emotionally, through playing than they do by sitting alone and filling in worksheets. They must believe that learning important concepts and skills does not occur through a linear progression of skill and drill exercises, one building on the other, with the whole edifice collapsing, like a tower of dominoes, if a child has not "mastered the next level."

Such teachers have to believe in the teacher's role as one of writing the script, designing the set, gathering the props, and stage managing the players—of providing the conditions for children's learning—rather than talking in order to "make deposits" into children's heads.

Teachers who choose this way must believe that building children's autonomy and independent functioning is a key educational goal that results as the teacher relinquishes control over student learning and provides them with more opportunities to choose and function by themselves. They must also believe that the cultivation of children's ability to think is one of education's primary functions and that, without having developed this ability, it is largely irrelevant that a child has learned to decode words, add and subtract sums, or "knows the answers" to the question in the science test about the temperature at which water boils.

Conversely, it is more than likely that instruction that centers on creative and investigative play will be anathema to those teachers whose perception of teaching and learning rests on the beliefs that

- teachers must be at center stage and in full control of every facet of student learning

- children must be quiet and orderly so that they may listen and do as they are told
- the teacher's most important job is to cover the content, which is sacrosanct at each grade level
- noisy, messy classrooms are a sure sign that children need to be properly disciplined
- silence means the children are learning
- learning is linear and sequential and must be meted out in a progressive series of tasks
- play is wasting time
- young children are unable to think for themselves

In other words, "What's important?" To choose play as a primary vehicle for learning, teachers and parents will, doubtless, decide on the merits of what's important for the healthful intellectual and emotional growth of children.

THE LAST WORDS

Many chapters in this book have been devoted to the importance of play for the healthful emotional and intellectual development of children. Not only is play "children's work," but it is also the avenue of creativity and invention. When children have become habituated to the wonders of creating, they become more autonomous and more able to create new and original opportunities to engage themselves productively and actively.

In other words, children who are "serious players" will rarely, if ever, have to sink into the despair of having "nothing to do." They are the ones least likely to suffer depression during stay-at-home days when schools are closed. Their creativity and inventiveness keep them occupied, happily, with little need for adult supervision and direction.

Now, in these last paragraphs, the wheel is turned toward the importance of play for healthful adulthood. On the one hand, one tends to dismiss play for adults as a trivial pursuit—perhaps a guilty pleasure. Something we shouldn't be doing because it takes us away from our more important, more serious tasks. But recent data reveal that play is just as significant for adults as it is for children.

In his book *Play*, Stuart Brown (2010), a medical doctor, writes that play shapes our brains, opens our imagination, and invigorates our souls. While the only kind of play we actually sanction for adults is competitive play, the need to be actively engaged as players helps us in untold ways—facilitating, for example, deeper connections between people, cultivating healing, improving human relationships. Play, Brown adds, strengthens mind, body, and spirit.

Yes, it is purposeless, fun, and pleasurable. Yes, the focus is on the experience and not on accomplishing a goal or "winning." But no matter the venue, a bit of play can go a long way toward boosting our productivity and happiness (Brown 2010). Drawing on research from around the world, Pink (2022) describes how play contributes to right brain development, why it has been sadly neglected in our educational experience, and why it is essential in preparing us to live in an uncertain future.

It is the work of Richard Feynman (1985) who provided us with an important insight into unfettered play, what on the surface looks to be silly, unproductive, and utterly without significance. He reminded us that play was the pivotal experience in enabling his thinking to move forward on the physics problem that eventually led to his winning the Nobel Prize. In his provocative and delightful book *Surely You're Joking Mr. Feynman* (1985), he writes that when his work in physics followed a structured pattern, he quickly became disgusted with it, no longer taking any pleasure from the work. So he taught himself to play with physics, doing whatever he felt like doing, because it was "interesting and amusing for me to play with."

In the cafeteria of Cornell University, much to the chagrin of his colleagues, Feynman played with dinner plates, actually tossing them up in the air and observing their "wobble rate." As he described it, "It was effortless. It was easy to play with those things. It was like uncorking a bottle. Everything flowed out effortlessly. I almost tried to resist it! There was no importance to what I was doing, but ultimately there was. The diagrams and the whole business that I got the Nobel Prize for came from that piddling around with the wobbling plates."

In the end there's no guarantee that playing will net any of the readers of this book a Nobel Prize. But it is hoped that the main thesis of this book has been more than borne out by the evidence that "the play's the thing."

References

Adam, Maureen. 1992. "The Responses of Eleventh Graders to Use of Case Method of Instruction in Social Studies." Master's thesis, Faculty of Education, Simon Fraser University.
Bettelheim, Bruno. 1987. "The Importance of Play." *Atlantic*, March 1987.
Brown, Stuart. 2010. *Play: How It Shapes the Brain, Opens the Imagination and Invigorates the Soul*. New York: Avery Books.
Bruner, Jerome. 1966. "On Teaching Thinking: An Afterthought." In *Thinking and Learning Skills*, vol. 2, ed. S. F. Chipman, J. W. Segal, and R. Glasser. Hillsdale, NJ: Erlbaum.
———. 1985. *On Knowing*. Cambridge, MA: Belknap Press.
Carkhuff, Robert R. 1969. *Helping and Human Relations*. Vol. 1. New York: Holt, Rinehart & Winston.
Dollard, John. 1939. *Frustration and Aggression*. New Haven, CT: Yale University Press.
Dunbar, H. Flanders. 1949. *Your Child's Mind and Body*. New York: Random House.
Ewing, David W. 1990. *Inside the Harvard Business School*. New York: Random House.
Featherstone, Joseph. 1971. *Schools Where Children Learn*. New York: Liveright.
Feynman, Richard. 1985. *Surely You're Joking Mr. Feynman*. New York: W. W. Norton.
Freire, Paolo. 1983. *Pedagogy of the Oppressed*. New York: Continuum.
French, Marilyn. 1985. *Beyond Power*. New York: Summit.
Gardner, Howard. 1991. *The Unschooled Mind*. New York: Basic Books.
Glasser, William. 1985. *Control Theory in the Classroom*. New York: HarperCollins.
Gordon, Mary. 2012. *Roots of Empathy: Changing the World, Child by Child*. Toronto: Thomas Allen.
Haidt, Jonathan. 2022. "After Babel: How Social Media Dissolved the Mortar of Society and Made America Stupid." *Atlantic*, May 2022.
Horwitz, Steven. 2015. "Cooperation over Coercion: The Importance of Unstructured Childhood Play for Democracy and Liberalism." *Cosmos + Taxis* 3(1):3–16.
Hubbard, Guy. 1987. *Art in Action*. San Diego: Coronado.

Isenberg, Joan, and Nancy Quisenberry. 1988. "Play: A Necessity for All Children." *Childhood Education* 24:138–45.

Kohn, Alfie. 1998. "Choices for Children: Why and How to Let Students Decide." *Phi Delta Kappan* 80:9–20.

Lansbury, Jane. 2022. "What If We Respected Toddlers as Whole People?" *New York Times*, February 15.

Piaget, Jean, and Barbel Inhelder. 1969. *The Psychology of the Child*. New York: Basic Books.

Pink, Daniel H. 2022. *A Whole New Mind*. New York: Riverhead Books.

Purkey, William. 1970. *Self Concept and School Achievement*. Englewood Cliffs, NJ: Prentice Hall.

Ramsey, Patricia. 1998. *Teaching and Learning in a Diverse World: Multicultural Education for Young Children*. New York: Teachers College Press.

Raths, Louis E. 1969. *Teaching for Learning*. Columbus, OH: Charles Merrill.

———. 1998. *Meeting the Needs of Children*. New York: Educator's International Press.

Reisman, David, Nathan Glazer, and Reuel Denney. 1953. *The Lonely Crowd*. New York: Doubleday.

Rogers, Carl. 1961. *On Becoming a Person*. Boston: Houghton Mifflin.

Seligman, Martin. 1991. *Learned Optimism*. New York: Knopf.

Spitz, Rene. 1949. "The Role of Ecological Factors in Emotional Development in Infancy." *Child Development* 20:145–56.

Walters, Alice. 1997. *Fanny at Chez Panisse*. New York: William Morrow Cookbooks.

Wassermann, Selma. 1987. "Teaching Strategies: Enabling Children to Develop Personal Power through Building Self Respect." *Childhood Education* 63(4):293–94.

———. 1991. "Theories of Empowerment." *Childhood Education* 67(4):235–39.

———. 2021. *Mastering the Art of Teaching*. Latham, MD: Rowman & Littlefield.

Wassermann, Selma, and J. W. George Ivany. 2022. *Science as Active Inquiry*. Latham, MD: Rowman & Littlefield.

Winchell, Paul. 1954. *Ventriloquism for Fun and Profit*. Baltimore: Ottenheimer.

Windschitl, Mark. 1999. "The Challenges of Sustaining a Constructivist Classroom." *Phi Delta Kappan* 80:751–55.

About the Author

Selma Wassermann is a professor emerita in the Faculty of Education at Simon Fraser University. She is the recipient of the University Award for Teaching Excellence. Her nineteen previous books include *Mastering the Art of Teaching* (2021), *Opening Minds* (2021), *Evaluation without Tears* (2020), *What's the Right Thing to Do?* (2019), *Teaching for Thinking Today* (2009), and *Case Method Teaching: A Guide to the Galaxy* (1994).

www.ingramcontent.com/pod-product-compliance
Lightning Source LLC
Chambersburg PA
CBHW020741230426
43665CB00009B/509